FIGHTING FOR AMERICA'S SOUL

How Sweeping Change Threatens Our Nation and What We Must Do

ROBERT H. KNIGHT

CORAL
RIDGE
MINISTRIES

Fort Lauderdale, Florida

CONTENTS

INTRODUCTION

Much has happened since the first edition of this book was published in June 2009. Suffice it to say that the political Left has been in the driver's seat and has been enacting as much of its agenda as possible before the American people get a chance to replace them. The magnitude of "change" in such a short amount of time is staggering.

Here is a short list of the most important developments. It's by no means exhaustive.

- The federal government essentially took over the nation's health care system when Barack Obama signed the 2,700-page Patient Protection and Affordable Care Act[1] of 2010 on March 23, 2010. The law requires all Americans to purchase health insurance or face a fine, and requires employers to offer health insurance or face fines. Twenty states have filed legal challenges, contending that the law is blatantly unconstitutional. Meanwhile, companies began shedding existing employee insurance programs in response to the new dictates, finding it cheaper to pay fines. And some insurers immediately began dropping certain coverage, such as for individual children. The Congressional Budget Office acknowledged that the law will cost far more than the claimed $900 billion price tag at the time of passage. For more, see Chapter 11.

- Obama signed the Matthew Shepard-James Byrd Jr. Hate Crimes Prevention Act of 2009,[2] a federal "hate crimes" law that lays the foundation for criminalizing Christian beliefs regarding sexual morality. Similar laws in Great Britain and Canada have led to outright suppression of any dissent from the view that sexual morality is a form of bigotry akin to racism, and that any resistance to the promotion of homosexuality constitutes an actionable offense.

- All federally backed college loans were placed under the authority of the Department of Education as of July 1, 2010, thus ending private college loan programs through banks.[3] This power grab was tucked into the ObamaCare bill[4] and got little publicity.

- The federal deficit ballooned to $1.5 trillion in fiscal 2010 and is projected to rise to $20.3 trillion (or 90 percent of Gross Domestic Product) by 2020, according to the Congressional Budget Office.[5]

- Two radical leftist ideologues—Sonia Sotomayor and Elena Kagan—were given lifetime appointments on the U.S. Supreme Court. Obama appointed many other radical judges to lower federal courts. For more on appointees, see Chapter 7.

- The Obama Administration and Congress moved toward ending the military's ban on homosexuality, despite pleas from all four Chiefs of the Armed Services to wait until a study was completed in December 2010. See more in Chapter 8.

- On July 8, 2010, a federal judge in Massachusetts struck down the federal Defense of Marriage Act (DOMA) after U.S. Solicitor General Elena Kagan made virtually no attempt to defend it.[6] In June 2010, Obama signed an order[7] granting marital benefits to same-sex partners of all federal employees, thus openly flouting DOMA, which defines marriage for all federal purposes and allows states to ignore claims that conflict with their own public policies regarding marriage. Obama, who claims to support man-woman marriage, has called for DOMA's repeal[8] and criticized as "unnecessary" California's Proposition 8, which amended the state Constitution to define marriage as the union of one man and one woman.[9] On Aug. 4, 2010, U.S. District Judge Vaughn Walker struck down the law, saying he could find no "rational basis" for defining marriage as the union of one man and one woman.[10]

- For the first time, the White House announced the exact number of nuclear missiles in America's arsenal in an astoundingly naïve bid to encourage our enemies to be similarly cooperative.[11]

- The House of Representatives passed on June 26, 2009, a Cap and Trade bill (The American Clean Energy and Security Act) that would create a monstrous system of federal agencies to assign "carbon credits" to businesses, shackling the private sector with mountains of new regulations and taxes.[12] Because the health care bill took months to pass, the Senate had yet to take action as of this writing. But the Environmental Protection Agency announced that it would treat carbon dioxide (yes, what we breathe out) as a pollutant and issue draconian carbon-limiting regulations on businesses.[13]

- On June 24, 2010, the House passed the DISCLOSE (Democracy Is Strengthened by Casting Light on Spending in Elections) Act, which would not only undo the Supreme Court's ruling striking down as unconstitutional the McCain-Feingold campaign restrictions on corporate and nonprofit entities, but would impose onerous new rules on corporations while allowing unions to spend freely on campaigns.[14] On July 27, however, the Senate in a party-line 41 to 57 vote rejected cloture on a GOP filibuster of the bill.[15] If enacted, the law would strangle opposition groups' ability to purchase political ads just prior to the congressional election in 2010 and again in the 2012 presidential election.

THE BIG PICTURE

The massive BP oil spill in the Gulf dominated the news in much of 2010, but another massive spill—of trillions of dollars—is still gushing out of control in Washington, D.C.

The Obama Administration and the Congress led by House Speaker Nancy Pelosi and Senate Majority Leader Harry Reid are spending staggering sums, while cobbling together government takeovers of one industry after another. The sheer magnitude of the changes has spooked many employers, who are reluctant to hire during a time when government is whipsawing the private sector with new demands almost daily. Unemployment continued to hover around 10 percent despite billions spent on make-work government jobs. "The private sector is scared stiff of what this guy is going to do

ONE

Violating the Right to Life

We hold these Truths to be self-evident,
that all Men are created equal, that they are endowed by
their Creator with certain unalienable Rights, that among
these are Life, Liberty and the Pursuit of Happiness.

DECLARATION OF INDEPENDENCE

The Constitution of the United States is the foundational document for America's legal system. However, it cannot properly be understood without examining it through the lens of the Declaration of Independence, which delineates the first principles of American law and liberty.

The Declaration says that our rights do not come from government, but from a Creator, and that the very first right is life itself. The Bible declares that man is made "in the image of God" (Genesis 1:27), which makes human life profoundly important. Thomas Jefferson, America's third president and the primary author of the Declaration of Independence, said, "The care of human life and happiness and not their destruction is the first and only legitimate object of good government."[1]

For centuries, even pagan societies have discouraged abortion as a moral wrong—the taking of an innocent human life. The Hippocratic Oath, which dates from the fourth century B.C. and from which our modern oath derives the dictum to physicians to "above all, do no harm," clearly prohibits abortion.

> I will not give a lethal drug to anyone if I am asked,
> nor will I advise such a plan; and similarly I will not
> give a woman a pessary to cause an abortion.[2]

But in 1964, Tufts University Academic Dean of Medicine Louis Lasagna wrote a modern version that removed the prohibition on euthanasia and abortion, and instead had this phrasing:

> Most especially must I tread with care in matters
> of life and death. If it is given me to save a life, all
> thanks. But it may also be within my power to take
> a life; this awesome responsibility must be faced
> with great humbleness and awareness of my own
> frailty. Above all, I must not play at God.[3]

The updated oath, according to PBS' *Doctors' Diaries* program, is used in many medical schools at graduation.[4] It leaves considerable room for doctors to commit both euthanasia and abortion.

Dr. D. James Kennedy and Jerry Newcombe observe in their book, *Lord of All*, that the abortion issue, perhaps more than any other, epitomizes the larger clash of values in our culture:

> Here is the conflict in its brutal simplicity: the
> Judeo-Christian concept of life vs. the humanistic,
> evolutionary view. The humanists may pride
> themselves on their creation of a new man, but
> make no mistake—take their perspective to the nth
> degree and you have one group of people deciding
> whether others should be able to live or die.[5]

HOW WE GOT HERE

For nearly the first 200 years of America's existence as a nation, the Judeo-Christian view prevailed, and abortion was widely considered a crime. Under English Common Law, the guiding force for American law until the early 1800s, abortion was illegal.[6] The English toughened their law in 1869, making abortion a felony. During the rest of the century, most of the U.S. states followed suit.[7]

In the early twentieth century, social reformer Margaret Sanger became active in the Eugenics Movement, which advocated the "improvement" of the human race via birth control, euthanasia of the "unfit," and eventually, abortion. Sanger went on to found Planned Parenthood, which campaigned for liberalized sales of birth control and then for abortion on demand. Planned Parenthood is now the largest abortion provider in the United States.

Sanger acquired a key ally when zoologist Alfred C. Kinsey published his groundbreaking study *Sexual Behavior in the Human Male* in 1948 and *Sexual Behavior in the Human Female* in 1953. Both books were based on thousands of interviews with people about their sex lives. Dr. Judith Reisman's and Edward Eichel's *Kinsey, Sex and Fraud* (1990) revealed Kinsey as a dishonest, promiscuous homosexual who manipulated and faked data to validate his own sexual adventures.[8] However, the research from the Kinsey Institute at Indiana University became the foundation for the American Law Institute's Model Penal Code for overhauling America's sexual laws.[9]

Former Planned Parenthood Medical Director Mary Calderone, a close Kinsey associate, cited the Kinsey data in her book, *Abortion in the United States* (1958), for her contention that "90 to 95 percent of pre-marital pregnancies are aborted." This absurd figure concerning abortion in the 1920s through the 1940s found its way into the ALI's Model Penal Code (ALI-MPC).

It was Kinsey's data, popularized by his co-authors and associates even after his death in 1956, that largely formed the misleading, positive picture of abortion that led to legalization.

In a 1958 book, *Sexual Behavior & the Law*, author Samuel Kling cites Kinsey:

> The Kinsey Institute reported that between one-fifth and one-fourth of the white married American women interviewed in their sample had had at least one induced abortion. Three-fourths of them reported no unfavorable consequences. Most did not regret the experience.[10]

There is not room here to cite all the problems with Kinsey's methodology, but one glaring fact should suffice: Kinsey could not induce enough married women to discuss their intimate sexual experiences, so he reclassified as "married" any woman living with a man for a year or more. This included prostitutes. Kinsey claimed that as many as one quarter of all married women had had physician-induced abortions, decades before abortion was decriminalized.

In 1959, again depending heavily on the Kinsey team's data, the ALI unveiled a model abortion code which called on states to ease their abortion laws.[11]

In 1967, Colorado, California, and North Carolina became the first states to legalize or liberalize abortion laws, followed by Georgia (1968), Maryland (1968), Delaware (1969), Arkansas (1969), Oregon (1969), New Mexico (1969), Virginia (1970), and South Carolina (1970). By 1970, when New York enacted the nation's most liberal abortion law, with abortion on demand up to 24 weeks of the pregnancy, 16 states allowed abortion, although 12 of them "were very restrictive, typically allowing abortion only for pregnancies due

Here's how *Washington Post* columnist Michael Gerson summarized the radical nature of the policies enacted and proposed by the new President and Congress:

> Americans disagree strongly about the proper legal status of abortion. But for decades there has been a rough consensus that no one should be compelled to participate in abortions or have their federal tax dollars used for abortion. These changes would shatter that consensus, making the destruction of life an essential part of the medical and legal order while stigmatizing and marginalizing all who object. This would be an outrage and a scandal—a troubling reinterpretation of religious liberty, which is not merely the freedom to believe, but the freedom to bring religiously informed moral beliefs to professional and public life.[4]

The "Mexico City Policy" barring use of federal tax dollars for international groups that promote or perform abortions was established in 1984 by President Ronald Reagan. President Bill Clinton abolished the policy in 1993, but President George W. Bush re-instituted it in 2001.

Now, in the twinkling of an eye, America has again gone from being an international moral force discouraging abortions to being a sugar daddy to International Planned Parenthood and other pro-abortion organizations.

There is more to come. On March 27, 2009, Planned Parenthood Federation gave Secretary of State Hillary Clinton the Margaret Sanger Award, named after Planned Parenthood's founder. In her speech at the Houston event, Clinton promised to reverse the Bush Administration's pro-life international policies.

Federal taxpayers will also have to pay to have embryonic humans used for research purposes and then destroyed. More than 70 treatments have already been developed from adult stem cells and umbilical cord blood, unlike embryonic cells, which still have not proved reliable. But politicians and the media, intent on promoting embryonic research, either neglect to cite the adult cell successes or they discuss them as if they came from embryonic research. The American people have been profoundly misled about this issue.

This move toward the creation of human life as a means to an end is not only immoral, but scientifically unnecessary.

In a March 4, 2009, column for *U.S. News & World Report*, Dr. Bernadine Healy, former director of the National Institutes of Health, said that

> Even for strong backers of embryonic stem cell research, the decision is no longer as self-evident as it was ... In fact, during the first six weeks of Obama's term, several events reinforced the notion that embryonic stem cells, once thought to hold the cure for Alzheimer's, Parkinson's, and diabetes, are obsolete. The most sobering: a report from Israel published in *PLoS Medicine* in late February that shows embryonic stem cells injected into patients can cause disabling if not deadly . . . [this case] is neither an anomaly nor a surprise, but one feared by many scientists.[5]

RESISTING THE ASSAULT ON HUMAN LIFE

In his remarkable 1983 essay, *Abortion and the Conscience of a Nation*, President Ronald Reagan wrote words that are equally powerful nearly three decades later:

Despite the formidable obstacles before us, we must not lose heart. This is not the first time our country has been divided by a Supreme Court decision that denied the value of certain human lives. The *Dred Scott* decision of 1857 was not overturned in a day, or a year, or even a decade. At first, only a minority of Americans recognized and deplored the moral crisis brought about by denying the full humanity of our black brothers and sisters; but that minority persisted in their vision and finally prevailed. They did it by appealing to the hearts and minds of their countrymen, to the truth of human dignity under God. From their example, we know that respect for the sacred value of human life is too deeply engrained in the hearts of our people to remain forever suppressed.[6]

To accomplish the return of a culture of life in which mothers and their babies would be respected and protected, he stressed the importance of first seeking God's guidance:

I have often said we need to join in prayer to bring protection to the unborn. Prayer and action are needed to uphold the sanctity of human life. I believe it will not be possible to accomplish our work, the work of saving lives, "without being a soul of prayer." The famous British Member of Parliament, William Wilberforce, prayed with his small group of influential friends, the "Clapham," for *decades* to see an end to slavery in the British empire. Wilberforce led that struggle in Parliament, unflaggingly, because he believed in the sanctity of human life. He saw the fulfillment of his impossible dream when Parliament outlawed slavery just before his death.[7]

To meet the current challenges to a culture of life, pro-life Americans need to

- Pray.
- Educate their friends and neighbors to the facts surrounding the issue of abortion.
- Support crisis pregnancy centers that aid women who choose to keep their babies, and even consider adopting children.
- Support public officials who put life ahead of political expediency. Voice their approval of pro-life legislation and their opposition to pro-abortion measures and policies.

THREE

Redefining Morality

A lot of Americans, especially those who have lived in the '30s and '40s, look around at our culture and wonder how it could have become so coarse. It did not happen overnight, but it did happen rapidly.

And it was no accident. Social revolutionaries have been hard at work for decades, undermining biblical values and supplanting them with Marxist-inspired materialism.

Much of the work has been accomplished through the universities and the arts—key institutions that transmit cultural values. Although Karl Marx himself believed that economics determined culture, one of his disciples, the Italian Antonio Gramsci, believed that culture determined economics. He set out to reform the world with the motto, "capture the culture."[1]

The word *culture* stems from *cult*, which means belief system, or religion. The clash between Judeo-Christian morality and atheist Marxism is really a clash of religions. Gramsci concluded that the arts and education could be used to infuse people with a new religion of socialism, which would eventually alter the economic and political landscape as well. Over the years, Marxist expatriates who fled Nazi Germany, such as playwright Bertolt Brecht, and the modernist Bauhaus architects and artists, exerted enormous influence on American culture.[2]

In his 1991 book *Capturing the Culture*, former *New York Times* correspondent and *Washington Times* columnist Richard Grenier revealed how Hollywood became a Gramscian dream when the Left, in effect, "captured" Tinseltown.[3] Grenier, a brilliant cultural commentator who died in 2002, noted that it was none other than Vladimir Lenin, the first dictator of Communist Russia, who said, "Of all the arts, for us cinema is the most important."[4] Lenin understood the visceral impact of sitting in a dark theater and viewing larger than life imagery while a soundtrack boomed.

As the twentieth century wore on, the arts, including cinema and television, became more and more sexualized, politicized, and hostile toward traditional values.

By the 1950s, America began changing rapidly from a Christian-based "ideational"[5] culture—one defined by pursuit of virtue that is informed by religious values—into a "sensate" culture, in which individuals seek pleasure at the expense of family, community, and ultimately, country.

Harvard sociologist Pitirim Sorokin saw the trend in America beginning even earlier and wrote about it in his book, *The Crisis of Our Age*, in 1941.

> Our culture simultaneously is a culture of man's glorification and of man's degradation. On the one hand, it boundlessly glorifies man and extols man-made culture and society. On the other, it utterly degrades the human being and all his cultural and social values. We live in an age which exalts man as the supreme end, and, at the same time, an age which vilifies man and his cultural values endlessly.[6]

What Sorokin called a "self-contradiction" was a secular mindset warring with the Judeo-Christian morality that had marked America since its founding. When man, instead of God, becomes the measure of all things, man will be worshipped at the same time that human life is cheapened. The humanist New Age view that man is ever evolving into a more perfect being results in individuals putting their own desires above God's laws and principles. When they do that, other human beings, such as unborn babies, can be seen as impediments to personal happiness.

In 1935, British anthropologist J.D. Unwin gave an address at Oxford that later became a book, *Sexual Regulations and Cultural Behaviour*. Unwin studied cultures throughout the ages and found that they waxed and waned depending on how much they valued monogamy:

> This type of marriage has been adopted by different societies, in different places, and at different times. Thousands of years and thousands of miles separate the events; and there is no apparent connection between them. In human records there is no case of an absolutely monogamous society failing to display great energy. I do not know of a case on which great energy has been displayed by a society that has not been absolutely monogamous.[7]

Societies that lose respect for marriage eventually lose creative energy derived from the kind of delayed gratification that strengthens families. Instead, people strive for immediate, sensory pleasures, and the societies become less dynamic and fertile.

Unwin found the pattern among the ancient Babylonians, Sumerians, the Romans and even "the English between the seventeenth and twentieth centuries." He said that these societies saw:

> ... the reduction of marriage to a temporary union made and broken by mutual consent. In some

cases, the demand for pre-nuptial (pre-marital) continence (abstinence) was also relaxed. It was in this manner that the sexual opportunity of these historical societies was extended; and, as soon as the lack of compulsory continence became part of the inherited tradition of a new generation, the energy of the society, or of a group within the society, decreased, and then disappeared.[8]

The decadent periods of Greece and Rome, which have been widely misrepresented as the apex of those civilizations instead of their nadirs, also reflect the pattern.

In 1956, Sorokin revisited the U.S. cultural scene in his book *The American Sexual Revolution,* comparing the sexualization of America to the decadent periods of Greek and Rome, as evidenced by the changes in art.

> During the early period of Greek and Roman culture, the rendered figures of their deities, heroes and mortals, especially those of women, were completely draped from head to foot: the Athena, Aphrodite, and Venus of this period were depicted as robust and chaste, without a trace of voluptuousness, as were also Zeus, Apollo, and even the serious young euphebus, Eros, and the bearded and garbed Dionysus, or Bacchus. If now and then a naked body was represented, its nudity was dryly hieratic, devoid of eroticism. Subsequently, in the decadent stages of these civilizations, the draperies began to slip off the shoulders of the Greek and Roman figures, until the Aphrodites and Dianas appeared in sexual nudity. Similarly, the

virile and impassive Apollo was transformed into the equivocal and sensual euphebus, the serious Eros into a play boy, the garbed Dionysus into an effeminate and erotic youth."[9]

Looking around in the 1950s at American literature, art, and film, Sorokin concluded that America was near the decadent stage that signaled the downfall of Rome and Greece.

In the '50s, America had a shockingly high 10 percent divorce rate and the launching of Hugh Hefner's pornography empire with *Playboy* magazine. Within a few short years, the media had popularized the bizarre Kinsey findings, the sex laws were loosened, and Hollywood and the publishing industry were fully aboard the campaign to turn the nation into Sodom and Gomorrah, or at least a Roman bath. During the '60s and '70s, the nation became awash in pornography, divorce, and a "gay" liberation movement that later embraced a "transgender" agenda and even sadistic sex in the twenty-first century.

Sorokin described the thriving business of pulp novels in the '50s this way:

> The world of this popular literature is a sort of human zoo, inhabited by raped, mutilated, and murdered females, and by he-males outmatching in bestiality any caveman and outlusting the lustiest of animals; male and female alike are hardened in cynical contempt of human life and values.[10]

In his book, *All Things Considered*, the early twentieth century British writer G.K. Chesterton observed that "sex is the materialist's religion." His point is that if people cease pursuing knowledge of God and God's rules for living, they turn to their appetites, and sex happens to be one of the most powerful.

In our time, if you spend even a few minutes scanning television programs, films, and pop music, you might conclude that sex, as Sorokin said decades earlier, is now America's religion.

Dr. D. James Kennedy and Jerry Newcombe point out in their book *Lord of All*,

> We practically never see a picture of a healthy family on television or in the movies. If there are pictures involving families, usually there are just bits and pieces. But if there is an entire family— one with a mother, father, and children—it is almost inevitably depicted as dysfunctional, grossly distorted, and unhappy. Today, if singles are portrayed, they are not pursuing anybody to the altar. If anything, they are running in the opposite direction. They are generally promiscuous, sex-crazed people.[11]

Imagine what Sorokin would think of the current cinema, TV shows, and row after row of porn magazines in mainstream bookstores. He might even note that even children's fare has degenerated, as evidenced by cleavage featured in Disney's *The Little Mermaid* (1989). One of the *Mermaid*'s creators told an interviewer that the team decided to "sexualize" Disney heroines and abandon the chaste model that characterized *Snow White* and *Cinderella*. By 2008, Disney's hit movie *Enchanted* had the heroine emerging from a shower in front of a man while clad only in a towel held by two helpful birds. It's an utterly gratuitous whiff of eros in an otherwise largely entertaining movie aimed at all ages.

As sex becomes what one Kinsey biographer described as "the measure of all things," it becomes increasingly difficult to hold

After threatening to disrupt the annual convention of the American Psychiatric Association and stacking the nomenclature committee with gay activists, the movement succeeded in having homosexuality removed in 1973 from the APA's *Diagnostic and Statistical Manual,* which describes psychological problems. As one pro-gay observer at the scene noted, the change came about not because of new science, but "was instead an action demanded by the ideological temper of the times."[1] Shortly thereafter, many professional groups, from the American Psychological Association to the nation's largest union, the two-million member National Education Association, began adopting pro-homosexual policies.

Working with the Kinsey-influenced American Law Institute, well-placed activists began weakening family laws throughout the nation, and began the drive to criminalize counseling and therapy for people who wish to overcome homosexual temptation.

They were aided by well-publicized, ultimately flawed studies that persuaded much of the public that people are "born gay" and cannot change. Therefore, organized homosexuality's drive for "rights" is identical to the legitimate aspirations of the black civil rights movement.

It didn't matter that none of these studies purporting to show a genetic tie to homosexuality was replicated and that many were exposed as junk science.[2] The media kept up the drumbeat with every new study and ignored later reports that called the data into question. Meanwhile, Hollywood did its part with an unending parade of sympathetic homosexual characters in films and on television, enforced by the advocacy group, Gays and Lesbians Against Defamation, which still routinely vets scripts.[3]

By 1993, Hawaii's Supreme Court, citing numerous now-questionable studies, ruled that the state's marriage law violated the state constitution's equal protection provision regarding "sexual orientation."[4]

BATTLE OVER MARRIAGE

The monumental battle over marriage quickly spread to the mainland, as Congress enacted the Defense of Marriage Act in 1996. Hawaiians rallied to defend marriage, and later passed a constitutional amendment in 1998 designating the legislature as the only authority that could define marriage law, which they then did. Alaska followed suit with its own constitutional amendment. More than 40 states strengthened their marriage laws or passed constitutional amendments defining marriage as only the union of one man and one woman.

Gay activists responded with a piecemeal strategy of persuading corporations, agencies, and legislators to designate some marital benefits for same-sex couples. It seemed harmless to many, so domestic partner policies began turning up in cities, states, and even in federal agencies, especially during the Clinton Administration.

At the U.S. Supreme Court, two key rulings have virtually dismantled the legal protections against the unraveling of society's sexual norms. In 1996, in *Romer v. Evans*, the court overturned Colorado's Amendment Two vote, which established a state law barring homosexuality from being equivalent to race in civil rights statutes.[5] In *Lawrence v. Texas* (2003), the court went further, striking down a Texas sodomy law and virtually declaring sodomy to be a constitutional "right." Majority opinion writer Justice Anthony Kennedy cited findings from international courts and the United Nations as part of the justification for overturning a law put in place by Texas legislators. In his dissent, Justice Antonin Scalia accused his colleagues of "taking sides in the culture war" and of reflecting an "anti-anti-homosexual" bias found throughout the nation's law schools.

Both majority opinions also heavily cite "findings" from various American professional associations that rely on flawed studies. Dr. Jeffrey Satinover, perhaps the most distinguished and credentialed they will be a graceful ornament on your head, and chains about your neck." (Proverbs 1:8, 9)

"Children, obey your parents in the Lord: for this is right. Honor your mother and father, which is the first commandment with promise; *that it may be well with thee, and thou may live long on the earth.*" And you, fathers, do not provoke your children to wrath, but bring them up in the training and admonition of the Lord." (Ephesians 6:1-4)

SOCIALIST VIEW OF MARRIAGE

According to the Bible, families are to take care of their own, with marriage as the foundation of the family. The socialist view of marriage is the polar opposite of the biblical model.

In his 1884 opus, *Origins of the Family, Private Property and the State*, Engels gives his dark historical view of marriage:

> … when monogamous marriage first makes its appearance in history, it is not as the reconciliation of man and woman, still less as the highest form of such a reconciliation. Quite the contrary. Monogamous marriage comes on the scene as the subjugation of the one sex by the other; it announces a struggle between the sexes unknown throughout the whole previous prehistoric period.[3]

Engels argued basically for "free love" as a byproduct of the advance of communism:

> With the transfer of the means of production into common ownership, the single family ceases to be the economic unit of society. Private housekeeping

is transformed into a social industry. The care and
education of the children becomes a public affair;
society looks after all children alike, whether they
are legitimate or not. This removes all the anxiety
about the "consequences," which today is the most
essential social—moral as well as economic—factor
that prevents a girl from giving herself completely
to the man she loves. Will not that suffice to
bring about the gradual growth of unconstrained
sexual intercourse and with it a more tolerant
public opinion in regard to a maiden's honor and a
woman's shame?[4]

Freed from any economic implications, Engels argues, women
and men will make up their own rules, liberated at last:

[T]hey will care precious little what anybody today
thinks they ought to do; they will make their own
practice and their corresponding public opinion
about the practice of each individual—and that will
be the end of it.[5]

America's "free love" movement in the 1960s could not have put
it any better.

Many socialists in Europe railed against the family as a
religiously-based, patriarchal brake on progress toward a classless
state. In the United States, their counterparts—liberals—have
worked for years to persuade Americans to surrender family functions
to outside parties. Part of the strategy was to shift the tax code
away from favoring families, as the Howard Center's Dr. Allan
Carlson explains:

★★ SIX ★★

The War on Private Charity

When it comes to serving the needy, there are two basic approaches. The first, inspired by Jesus Himself and required in the Old Testament, is sacrificial giving of oneself. This has been the cornerstone of American charity since the nation's founding, and it remains the most effective way to assist the poor.

Another, diametrically opposite approach is socialism, in which income is forcibly seized and then redistributed to groups and individuals favored by government officials. Socialism is rooted in the formula from Karl Marx—"from each according to his ability to each according to his needs." That is a fine arrangement when voluntary, such as in families, churches, and private charities. However, when it is imposed by force—and socialism is always accompanied by force since it violates human nature—it is soft tyranny masquerading as charity.

Since the 1930s, with the advent of the New Deal, the federal government, along with local and state governments, have taken on more and more functions that previously were handled by families, churches, and private charities.

Social Security, the largest government income transfer program, was originally aimed at assisting intact families. Now, it is an ever growing tax on employees and employers that has driven a wedge between the generations. How? Because in centuries past, parents had more children partly to fulfill the biblical mandate to "be fruitful and multiply," but also as a way to insure that someone would provide for them in their old age.

Social Security removed the advantage of having children, since it guarantees income based solely on age (and previous employment). Someone who has no children gets the same amount as someone who had 10 children who grew up to pay into the system, thus supporting the childless retiree. Children are very expensive, as any parent can tell you. Social Security makes having them less advantageous, economically. Of course, many people will attest that Social Security has allowed millions of older Americans to live in at least minimally comfortable circumstances. But the other social effects are not often voiced or acknowledged.

The same can be said about Medicare, Medicaid, and many other enormous federal programs. The advantages are obvious, but the downsides are not so obvious. To pay for all this, the average American family's tax burden has risen from a mere 2 percent of income in 1948[1] to nearly 30 percent[2], when all taxes are accounted for. This has forced many mothers into the workplace who would, all things being equal, rather spend the time raising their children. Consequently, this has created a huge market for paid childcare, with the government subsidizing it via tax credits and in some cases through direct payments. Thus, families are paying taxes to create a system that offers incentives for them to spend less time with their own children. While this may delight feminists, who want all women to pursue careers instead of homemaking, it makes it harder for families that opt for a different model.

$5.7 BILLION FOR "PAID" VOLUNTEERS

On April 21, 2009, President Obama signed the "Edward M. Kennedy Serve America Act" bill, tripling the size of the federal government's paid "volunteer" programs, including AmeriCorps. The plan calls for spending $5.7 billion over the next five years and $10 billion over the next 10 years, and putting 250,000 paid "volunteers" on the government payroll.

Generosity has been a hallmark of American character. It's a product of the nation's Judeo-Christian heritage, and it's the polar opposite of cold, contractual transfers that characterize socialism. In fact, socialism is so ugly in practice that it has to destroy its competitor, private charity, hence the proposed assault on charitable tax deductions.

Some of the largest secular groups in America, such as the AARP, enthusiastically supported the Kennedy Act boondoggle. They stand to gain paid "volunteers" at the expense of smaller competitors, such as churches.

Faith-based charities are technically eligible, but will get squeezed out by "nondiscrimination" language. In practice, this means that a Catholic-run homeless shelter would have to employ atheists or Buddhists. The Salvation Army, perhaps the most effective charity, requires volunteers—not its clients—to adhere to Christian beliefs. Because of that, the Army will be shut out from employing any of the government's paid "volunteers."

Why would anyone think that government involvement would improve volunteerism? On the Senate floor, Sen. Jim DeMint (R-S.C.) warned:

> ...Our history shows us when Government gets involved, it tends to take something that is working and make it not work nearly as well. Civil society works because it is everything Government is not. It is small, it is personal, it is responsive, it is accountable. Civil society must be protected from any effort to make it more like Government. This bill centralizes control of important functions of our civil society.

MANDATORY CIVILIAN SERVICE?

The original bill called for creating a commission to study mandatory civilian service, but that was yanked amid public outcry. However, it has re-emerged in H.R. 1444, the "Congressional Commission on Civil Service Act," sponsored by Washington Rep. Jim McDermott (D).

This free-standing bill, which directs the proposed commission to "enhance our Nation and the global community," reaches to kid-level, providing "the means to develop awareness of national service and volunteer opportunities at a young age by creating, expanding and promoting service options for primary and secondary school students."

If you think this will be limited to public schools, you don't know the mindset driving this bus.

And if you're a sacrificial parent homeschooling or sending your children to a religious school so that they won't be engulfed by the public school MTV culture that has led 11-year-olds to "sex text" nude pictures to each other, you'll be out of luck. Your kid will need to go with the flow.

The McDermott bill requires the commission to study "[w]hether a workable, fair, and reasonable mandatory service requirement for all able young people could be developed to … overcome civic challenges by bringing together people from diverse economic, ethnic, and educational backgrounds." Or, as riot icon Rodney King might say, "Can't we all be *forced* to get along?"

On the face of it, mandatory civilian service violates the 13th Amendment's prohibition on involuntary servitude. During a national crisis, such as World War II, married men with children were given the choice: military service or work in a defense plant. The Constitution's Article 1, Section 8, allows Congress to "raise and support armies" and to "provide and maintain a navy." It's one thing to allow for conscientious objection to a military draft; it's another to draft civilians to serve in politicians' pet projects absent an emergency.

The McDermott bill also charges the commission with examining "the need" for a federal four-year college to train "future public sector leaders."

Think of it, an entire university churning out graduates with the same mentality as ACORN, which is to say that they will view the nation as entirely secular and public, except the parts that are stubbornly and temporarily private.

President Obama has also proposed cutting tax deductions for private charity for the wealthiest givers. Harvard economics Prof. Martin Feldstein warned in a *Washington Post* column that this could severely hurt nonprofits:

> President Obama's proposal to limit the tax deductibility of charitable contributions would effectively transfer more than $7 billion a year from the nation's charitable institutions to the federal government. ... In effect, the change would be a tax on the charities, reducing their receipts by a dollar for every dollar of extra revenue the government collects. ...With the endowments of charitable institutions sharply reduced by the fall in stock prices, this loss of gifts would make an already bad situation worse.[3]

The proposal, which would take effect in 2011, would trim the amount that people could deduct. It would apply to married couples with incomes of more than $250,000 and single people with incomes greater than $200,000.

The administration's plan would limit the amount

that high-income individuals could deduct to 28 percent of their gifts, down from 35 percent, even though their incomes would still be taxed at a higher marginal rate. This raises the cost per dollar of giving from 65 cents to 72 cents, an increase of 10.8 percent that can be expected to reduce the total giving of these donors by about 10 percent.[4]

Taken together, the massive increase in government aid to paid "volunteers" and the reduced incentive for charitable giving is a double-barreled shotgun aimed at traditional giving in the private sector.

The biggest loser will be faith-based charities, since the law expanding AmeriCorps and other programs will exclude any charity that "discriminates" on the basis of religious belief. In effect, the government is bribing volunteers to cease helping churches and faith-based charities by creating a paid competitor.

The immediate answer might seem to be to say, "Well, don't take any government money then." That's sound advice. But by funding largely secular groups, the government skews the market against faith-based charities, which is exactly what socialists have wanted to do for years.

Americans need to stand by the faith-based charities whose own government is creating competition for volunteers. People need to consider giving more and to volunteer their time.

They also need to let their elected representatives know that these assaults on charities cannot be allowed to stand. No wrongful policy is irreversible when enough citizens are aroused to take action.

SEVEN

Stacking the Deck
With Radical Appointees

One of the president's most important powers is that of making appointments of judges and executives of federal agencies. Judges, especially, can shape the legal and political landscape years after the administration has left office.

ELENA KAGAN—SOLICITOR GENERAL, U.S. SUPREME COURT JUSTICE

On March 31, 2009, Elena Kagan became Solicitor General of the United States, the second most powerful legal authority. With "yes" votes from seven Republicans, the Senate affirmed her 61 to 31 on March 19. She was then nominated on May 10, 2010, to replace the retiring Associate Justice John Paul Stevens on the U.S. Supreme Court. Despite Kagan's lack of judicial experience and a voluminous record of favoring left-wing judicial activism, the Senate voted 63 to 37 on August 5, 2010, to place her on the High Court.

As an advisor in the Clinton White House, Kagan formulated the legal rationale for partial birth abortion. Her conduct, as revealed during her Senate hearing and related here by a *Washington Times* editorial, should be beyond the pale:

> Documents from Ms. Kagan's service in Bill Clinton's administration show her saying it would

be a "disaster" if word got out that the American College of Obstetricians and Gynecologists (ACOG) "could identify no circumstances under which [the partial-birth procedure] ... would be the only option to save the life or preserve the health of the woman." She was so ideologically committed to keeping partial-birth abortions legal that she didn't want the full medical truth released without accompanying language that diluted the impact of the facts. In another memo, Ms. Kagan laments that it was "a problem" that Mr. Clinton might want to restrict such abortions to a greater degree than she did.

Ms. Kagan took it upon herself to draft language for ACOG to insert into its findings, and then she had the gall to present the amended statement to the president without acknowledging that it had been altered, for political reasons, at her direction. Ms. Kagan drafted language stating that partial-birth abortion "may be the best or most appropriate procedure in a particular circumstance." This later became the linchpin of lower court fact-finding and the Supreme Court's decision (largely reversed a decade later) that a ban on partial-birth abortions was unconstitutional. Without the language, those particularly inhumane abortions would have been banned a decade earlier.[1]

As Harvard Law School dean, Kagan filed a brief with the U.S. Supreme Court seeking to overturn the Solomon Amendment, which requires colleges accepting federal funds to allow military recruiters. Kagan wants the military to open its ranks and barracks to homosexuals, and did considerable activism on behalf of Harvard's homosexual groups.

Political analyst Andrew C. McCarthy writes:

> At Harvard, Dean Kagan's gay-rights activism was as limitless as her pro-abortion activism had been. She banned on-campus military recruitment. Doing so was a flagrant violation of federal law, but she rationalized it by her moral outrage over the armed forces' "Don't Ask, Don't Tell" policy.[2]

Kagan threw military recruiters off campus immediately after a federal court in another jurisdiction ruled against the recruiters. But she had no problem with Harvard accepting $20 million from a Saudi Royal Family member to start a center for Islamic Studies and Shariah law.[3] In 2003, she presided over the establishment of an Islamic Finance Project at Harvard Law School itself. As Frank Gaffney of the Center for Security Policy explains, "The Project's purpose is to promote what is better known as 'Shariah-Compliant Finance (SCF) by enlisting in its service some of the nation's most promising law students."[4] The idea is to bring all financial institutions under the service of Sharia Law and thus usher in a Sharia-compliant society.

As Solicitor General, Kagan was responsible for all litigation on behalf of the United States in the Supreme Court and federal appellate courts, and began using her enormous authority to help unravel the moral order. She made ridiculously weak arguments in defending the military's ban on homosexuality and also in a case involving the Defense of Marriage Act (DOMA). In the latter, the U.S. government declined to present any evidence that marriage might be important to children's well being despite a mountain of research to that effect. I think it's fair to say that she helped sabotage

DOMA, not defend it.

The rest of this chapter is not an exhaustive list of President Obama's major executive appointees, but highlights a few to illustrate the radical bent of the administration. For a more detailed look, see my book *Radical Rulers: The White House Elites Who Are Pushing America Toward Socialism*, Coral Ridge Ministries, 2010, at www. radicalrulers.com).

In the Coral Ridge Ministries booklet *All the President's Men & Women: The People and Politics of the Obama Administration*, Jennifer Kennedy Cassidy writes in the foreword that,

> Judged purely by their professional qualifications, the Obama nominees are an impressive lot, coming in many cases from the best schools and bringing long years of professional and/or political experience. But judged by their policy preferences, the men and women who will sit in the Cabinet Room with President Obama tilt toward the left and away from the values and virtues embraced by pro-family evangelicals.[5]

U. S. DISTRICT JUDGE DAVID HAMILTON

Barack's Obama's first judicial appointee was U.S. District Judge David Hamilton to the Seventh Circuit Court of Appeals. Hamilton had struck down an Indiana law requiring a waiting period for abortions and also ruled against a "sectarian" Christian prayer opening the state legislature. His ruling was overturned by the very same court to which he has been appointed. Led by the *New York Times*, which parroted the administration's press handouts, the media promptly misidentified Hamilton as a "moderate."[6] A GOP Senate filibuster was crushed 70 to 29, with Hamilton confirmed on a 59-39 vote.

GOVERNOR KATHLEEN SEBELIUS—
DEPARTMENT OF HEALTH AND HUMAN SERVICES

At the Department of Health and Human Services, the largest federal agency outside of the Defense Department, Obama appointed as secretary, Kansas Gov. Kathleen Sebelius (D), one of the most pro-abortion public officials in America. Sebelius ran into some problems with her nomination when it was revealed that she had understated donations to her campaign by Wichita's George Tiller, the nation's most notorious late-term abortionist. Sebelius has spoken at Planned Parenthood functions and also backed the kind of sweeping government takeover of health care championed by Hillary Clinton. The Senate confirmed her on April 28, 2009, by a vote of 65 to 31, which included nine Republicans, among whom was fellow Kansan and outspoken pro-lifer Sam Brownback.

NANCY SUTLEY—COUNCIL ON ENVIRONMENTAL QUALITY

For chairman of the Council on Environmental Quality, Obama appointed Nancy Sutley, who held a variety of environmental posts and was also a member of Hillary Clinton's California Lesbian, Gay, Bisexual and Transgender primary steering committee.

M. JOHN BERRY—OFFICE OF PERSONNEL MANAGEMENT

Over at the Office of Personnel Management, which oversees 1.9 million federal employees, and 2.5 million retirees and survivor annuitants, Obama nominated M. John Berry, the openly homosexual director of the National Zoo. Berry initiated a number of pro-homosexual employee policies during his zoo tenure.

On June 1, 2010, as OPM director, Berry announced that same-sex partners of federal employees would be eligible for long-term disability benefits. On June 2, 2010, Obama announced that a whole range of marital-type benefits, including adoption counseling, access to fitness facilities, medical treatment, credit unions, hardship transfer considerations and several others would be extended to same-sex partners. In a June 2 memorandum, Berry ordered all executive agencies to implement the new policies.[7] The move is a blatant bypassing of the federal Defense of Marriage Act,[8] which defines marriage for all federal purposes as the union of one man and one woman.

In a press release, Berry hailed the moves: "This is another major step forward for gay and lesbian federal employees."[9]

STEVEN CHU—SECRETARY OF ENERGY

For Secretary of Energy, Obama tapped Steven Chu, a 1997 Nobel Prize winner for his work with lasers. However, Dr. Chu is also an aggressive backer of the more extreme theories of global warming and has predicted catastrophic outcomes if carbon emissions are not curbed. Here is an excerpt from Fox News, reporting on Chu's speech at the Summit of the Americas on April 18, 2009, where Chu predicted that oceans would rise, islands would disappear, and the United States would suffer as well:

> "Lots of area in Florida will go under. New Orleans at three-meter height is in great peril. If you look at, you know, the Bay Area, where I came from, all three airports would be under water. So this is—this is serious stuff. The impacts could be enormous." Conservative climate change skeptics immediately denounced Chu's assessment of the threat and potential consequences of global warming.
>
> "Secretary Chu still seems to believe that computer model predictions decades or 100 years

from now are some sort of 'evidence' of a looming climate catastrophe," said Marc Morano, executive editor of ClimateDepot.com and former top aide to global warming critic Sen. Jim Inhofe, R-Okla.

"Secretary Chu's assertions on sea level rise and hurricanes are quite simply being proven wrong by the latest climate data. As the Royal Netherlands Meteorological Institute reported in December 12, 2008: There is 'no evidence for accelerated sea-level rise.'"

Morano said hurricane activity levels in both hemispheres of the globe are at 30-year lows and hurricane experts like MIT's Kerry Emanuel and Tom Knutson of the National Oceanic and Atmospheric Administration "are now backing off their previous dire predictions."[10]

TIMOTHY GEITHNER—TREASURY SECRETARY

For Treasury Secretary, the president picked Timothy Geithner, president of the Federal Reserve Bank of New York. Geithner, like several other nominees, faced embarrassing scrutiny when personal tax problems surfaced.[11] He has championed massive federal intervention into the financial system, including the takeover of several banks and taxpayer bailout of General Motors, insurance giant AIG and financiers Bear Stearns. Although the $787 billion "stimulus" package failed to reduce the unemployment rate, which increased to around 10 percent during 2010, Geithner has argued for additional government make-work expenditures.

At the Justice Department, the president has picked a team from the top down that is far to the left of the American public. Given its enormous responsibilities to uphold or undermine the nation's laws, the DOJ's lineup should worry even self-styled liberals.

ERIC HOLDER—ATTORNEY GENERAL

For the nation's top law enforcer, Obama chose Eric Holder, a deputy attorney general under Bill Clinton who, upon taking office as top Justice official, promptly criticized his fellow citizens for not discussing racial matters more, calling America "a nation of cowards."[12] Holder supported passage of the federal hate crimes legislation that includes "sexual orientation" and builds the foundation for similar laws in Europe and Canada that have resulted in suppressing the freedoms of religion, speech, and assembly. His Justice Department sued the state of Arizona on July 6, 2010, because of Arizona's law requiring police to check immigration status during legal stops and arrests.[13] The Justice Department also failed to prosecute two members of the New Black Panther Party who had been caught on videotape harassing voters at a Philadelphia polling place in 2008. Justice Department attorney J. Christian Adams resigned over the decisions and testified before the U.S. Civil Rights Commission that Justice Department attorneys have been told not to pursue any cases involving minority defendants.[14] Holder also insisted on bringing terrorists from Guantanamo Bay for trial in U.S. civilian courts, a decision met with considerable hostility in New York City, where the destruction of the World Trade Center in 2001 killed nearly 3,000 people.

Other Justice Department appointees in top positions have been making it resemble "Happy Hour" at the Kinsey Institute.

DAVID OGDEN—DEPUTY ATTORNEY GENERAL

David Ogden has a long record of serving the porn and abortion industries and the radical homosexual lobby. He even filed a brief defending a child pornographer in a 1993 case that got Attorney General Janet Reno reprimanded by both houses of Congress.

Ogden's nomination as Deputy Attorney General sailed through the Senate on March 12 with a vote of 65-28, aided by 11 Republicans, including presidential nominee John McCain, South Carolina's Lindsey Graham, and Ohio's George Voinovich. After a short stint at Justice, Ogden resigned on Dec. 3, 2009, citing differences with his superiors. But the fact that he made the cut in the first place speaks volumes about the values of the Obama Administration and those of many senators.

Sen. Patrick Leahy (D-Vt.), who spoke on Ogden's behalf, said Ogden's legal work on behalf of the smut industry was just a "sliver" of his record and, in any case, did not reflect his "personal" views or values. It's doubtful that lawyers working for corporate polluters or pro-life groups would get that kind of pass.

It's hard to imagine a more radical nominee in terms of legal social engineering.

On November 4, 1993, in a vote of 100 to 0, the U.S. Senate passed a non-binding resolution censuring the Justice Department for refusing to defend the conviction of a child pornographer. In that case, *Knox v. United States,* Ogden had filed a friend of the court brief for the ACLU that argued that close-ups of children's crotches in videos such as "Little Girl Bottoms (Underside)" and "Little Blondes" were not child pornography and thus merited constitutional protection. A week later, President Clinton issued a letter rebuking Attorney General Janet Reno and asking for tougher child pornography enforcement. A few months later, the House added its censure by a vote of 425 to 3.

If this had been an isolated incident, which Mr. Ogden now regrets, that would be one thing, but he has a long track record of siding with radical proponents of the sexual revolution.

Brian Burch, president of the Catholic-based public policy group Fidelis, outlined Ogden's extensive career issuing briefs on behalf of the ACLU, pornographers, abortionists, and homosexual pressure groups. Here are a few of Mr. Ogden's activities:

- Opposed the Children's Internet Protection Act of 2000. Ogden filed an amicus brief arguing against Congress requiring public libraries that accept tax funding to install Internet filters.
- Challenged the Child Protection and Obscenity Enforcement Act of 1988. Specifically, Ogden's brief on behalf of porn producers argued that requiring them to verify that performers were at least 18 years of age would "burden too heavily and infringe too deeply" on their First Amendment rights.
- Represented Playboy Enterprises in a 1986 suit that forced the Library of Congress to print *Playboy* magazine's articles in Braille, an outcome that Ogden said was a key victory in "turning the tide in the censorship battle." He also sought an injunction against *Playboy's* inclusion in a list of porn magazines that were to be included in the Meese Commission report (1990).
- Filed numerous briefs in other pornography and obscenity cases before the Supreme Court.
- Opposed parental notification for minors undergoing abortions (1987).
- Opposed virtually all restrictions on abortions, from spousal notification to mandatory 24-hour delays, in a brief for Planned Parenthood filed in the landmark *Casey v. Planned Parenthood* (1992).
- Characterized peaceful pro-life abortion protesters as the moral equivalent of mobsters by

arguing that they come under the RICO organized crime statute (*Scheidler v. National Organization for Women*—2003).

- Declared that "homosexuality is a normal form of human sexuality" as counsel for the American Psychological Association in *Lawrence v. Texas* (2003), in which the Supreme Court struck down the Texas sodomy law. That profoundly bold judicial power grab has been the linchpin for further gay rights advances, including state court rulings striking down marriage laws in Massachusetts, California, and Connecticut.
- Sought to overturn the military's policy on service by open homosexuals (*Watkins v. United States Army* (1989), arguing that sexual preference (sexual orientation) is the equivalent of race.

Mr. Ogden has also backed the intrusion of international law into American courts, the "right" of protesters to trespass on private property, the use of "compassion" to override "precedent and logic," and he has filed several briefs seeking to limit enforcement of the death penalty. His briefs are littered with junk science that was specifically designed to undermine cultural norms.

DAWN JOHNSEN—ASSISTANT ATTORNEY GENERAL NOMINEE

Obama nominated Dawn Johnsen to be Assistant Attorney General, running the Office of Legal Counsel. Johnsen was a staff counsel for the ACLU and legal director for the National Abortion and Reproductive Rights Action League (NARAL). In 1989, in a friend of the court brief in *Webster v. Reproductive Health Services*,

Johnsen equated having a baby with slavery:

> Statutes that curtail [a woman's] abortion choice
> are disturbingly suggestive of involuntary servitude,
> prohibited by the Thirteenth Amendment in that
> forced pregnancy requires a woman to provide
> continuous physical service to the fetus in order to
> further the state's asserted interest.[15]

As *The Washington Times* observed in an editorial:

> The Thirteenth Amendment to the Constitution
> abolished slavery in 1865. The statute Ms. Johnsen
> opposed was written to limit public funding for
> abortions. It takes a questionable leap in logic
> to argue that involuntary servitude results from
> taxpayer funds not being used for abortion. Even
> if a woman cannot afford an abortion, the choice
> to have sex was her own, and that involved the
> possibility of getting pregnant. Taxpayers had
> nothing to do with her sexual choices and are not
> enslaving her by preferring that their money not
> be used to end her baby's life.[16]

The Times also noted that during her hearing, Johnsen denied
that she had ever made a Thirteenth Amendment argument and
had made other claims that lacked evidence. After her radical record
became public knowledge, Johnsen's nomination sat on the shelf
until she herself withdrew in on April 9, 2010.

THOMAS PERRELLI—ASSOCIATE ATTORNEY GENERAL

Obama also nominated Thomas Perrelli to be Associate
Attorney General. Perrelli was the lawyer for Michael Schiavo,

who had his brain-damaged wife Terri taken off life support against the wishes of her brother and parents. Perrelli was confirmed by the Senate on March 12, 2009.

GOODWIN LIU—NINTH CIRCUIT NOMINEE.

In February 2010, Obama nominated Goodwin Liu, a UC Berkeley law professor, to the U.S. Court of Appeals for the Ninth Circuit.[17] Mr. Liu testified in 2006 against Samuel Alito's Supreme Court appointment. In March, 2010, 42 of California's 58 district attorneys signed a letter urging the Senate Judiciary Committee to reject Liu, stating, "his views on criminal law, capital punishment, and the role of the federal courts in second-guessing state decisions are fully aligned with the judges who have made the Ninth Circuit the extreme outlier that it presently is."[18]

In a book Liu co-authored, Keeping Faith with the Constitution, he wrote that "evolving norms and traditions of our society" should be the key to interpreting the Constitution. He also joined an amicus brief arguing that the equal protection clause contains a "right" to same-sex marriage. During a Senate Judiciary Committee hearing on April 16, 2010, Liu said, "Whatever I've written in books and articles would have no bearing on my role as a judge."[19] On May 13, 2010, the Senate Judiciary Committee voted 12 to 7 on party lines to advance Mr. Liu's nomination to the full Senate.[20]

Despite ongoing rhetoric about unifying the nation, the Obama Administration has put into place an executive and judicial team that is sharply to the left of most Americans, especially those who are pro-life, pro-marriage, pro-free market, and who hold other traditional moral values.

EIGHT

Disarming the Armed Forces With Social Experimentation

O ne of the Left's most ambitious goals is to transform the nation's armed forces into a petri dish for their most radical social experiments. According to Gallup's 2010 Confidence in Institutions poll,[1] the military ranks at the top, with 76 percent expressing approval. No wonder the radicals want to plant a rainbow flag atop the Pentagon.

By contrast, the increasingly radical Congress ranked at the bottom, with only 11 percent saying they had "a great deal" or "quite a lot of confidence" in the lawmakers.

In 1993, after Bill Clinton was elected president, one of the first things he did was to announce that he would end the military's ban on homosexuality.

> Army Col. (ret.) David Hackworth, the most decorated living veteran, wrote, "I cannot think of a better way to destroy fighting spirit and gut U.S. combat effectiveness."[2]

Clinton's announcement unleashed a major political and cultural battle that ended with Congress passing a law preserving the ban.

Noting that the new law[3] dropped the question about homosexuality at recruits' induction, the Clinton administration developed an implementation policy called "Don't Ask, Don't Tell." This rule allows homosexuals to serve as long as they keep their preference confidential. The actual law, however, which has been upheld in every court case, specifically bars anyone with even the "propensity" for homosexuality.

Over the years, the "Don't Ask, Don't Tell" policy became synonymous with the law. As in years past, hundreds of men and women have been discharged annually for admitting to homosexual acts or getting caught.

The American public seemed satisfied that the armed forces had not been seriously compromised, so nothing was done to repair the breach between the law and the policy.

Meanwhile, the ACLU and homosexual activist groups like the Service Members Legal Defense Network campaigned to change public opinion via a series of legal cases, polls, biased studies, and relentless media coverage of personal interest stories, all geared to recast this falsely as a "civil rights" issue and away from military necessity.

Homosexual activists, including the director of the Palm Center at the University of California at Santa Barbara, a pro-homosexual think tank often cited by the media as an objective source of data about the issue, assembled a list in November 2008 of about 100 former senior officers who said they think the ban should be lifted.[4] The media gave them extensive coverage and began airing more and more stories about the "inevitability" of the ban's demise.

Fast forward to 2009: With the election of Barack Obama and a radical Congress, the Left felt emboldened to try to do what seemed unthinkable only a few years before.

On the White House Web site, President Obama included repealing "Don't Ask, Don't Tell" as one of the stated "civil rights" objectives of his administration.[5]

On March 3, 2009, Rep. Ellen Tauscher (D-Calif.) introduced

the absurdly titled Military Readiness Enhancement Act of 2009,[6] which would repeal the 1993 law. The next year, Rep. Patrick Murphy (D-Pa.) took over as chief sponsor when Tauscher resigned her seat.

By 2010, the Pentagon, as represented by Defense Secretary Robert Gates and Joint Chiefs of Staff Chairman Admiral Michael Mullen, signaled their readiness to cave in to homosexual—and the Obama White House's—demands. They authorized a study to be done by December 2010 including a survey of military personnel about how—not whether—to implement the repeal of the policy. Still, Congress, even with the chiefs of the four services, plus Gates and Mullen, asking them to wait until the study was completed, moved ahead with the legislation. Who cares what people in the armed services think, even in time of war?

Meanwhile, resistance continued to grow, and the bill was deemed too hot to put on the floor for a stand-alone vote. So on May 28, 2010, the bill was added as an amendment to a defense reauthorization bill, which the House passed by a vote of 234 to 194.[7] The Senate Armed Services Committee also approved the bill with the repeal in it. But the measure had yet to come to the full Senate as of this writing, and Sen. John McCain (R-Ariz.) pledged to lead a filibuster if the repeal was not stricken from the bill.

Forbidden to take sides in political battles, servicemen and women have had to stay on the sidelines while their fate is decided. The few people brave enough to support the military's policy in public have come in for rough treatment.

When Center for Military Readiness President Elaine Donnelly testified before the House Armed Services Committee on July 23, 2008, on behalf of keeping the ban, she was interrupted, assailed, and mocked by liberal Members from both parties. The next day, *Washington Post* columnist Dana Milbank savaged Donnelly,[8] utterly misrepresenting what occurred at the hearing. At one point he described her testimony, which tapes clearly reveal as unruffled and professional, as "an extraordinary exhibition of rage."

Milbank's column epitomizes the kind of abuse that the media give anyone who opposes any portion of the homosexual political and cultural agenda.

For their part, congressmen on the panel behaved just as badly: "just bonkers" (Rep. Vic Snyder, D-Ark.), "embarrassed," (Rep. Carol Shea-Porter, D. N.H.), and "shocked," (Rep. Ellen Tauscher, D-Calif.).

"What they've done is make my point," Donnelly said after the hearing, "which is that if the ban is lifted, people who believe in traditional sexual morality will be abused and have no recourse, no defenders."[9] Retired Army Ranger Sgt. Brian Jones, the lone witness to testify in support of Donnelly's position, and who also calmly made his case, met similar derision.

An important point to remember about the military is that it is not like civilian service, where people can go home after work. Soldiers and sailors live together 24 hours a day, often in very close proximity.

"Lifting the ban would amount to forced co-habitation with homosexuals," Donnelly said.

Donnelly for months was virtually the only defender of the military policy in many media interviews. But on March 31, 2009, the cavalry rode in with flags flying and guns blazing. More than 1,000 retired generals and admirals under the auspices of Flag and General Officers for the Military[10] signed a letter to Congress and the President urging them not to open the armed forces to open homosexuality. By July 2010, that number had risen to 1,161, including more than 50 four-star officers.

The letter reads in part:

> Our past experience as military leaders leads us to
> be greatly concerned about the impact of repeal [of

the law] on morale, discipline, unit cohesion, and overall military readiness. We believe that imposing this burden on our men and women in uniform would undermine recruiting and retention, impact leadership at all levels, have adverse effects on the willingness of parents who lend their sons and daughters to military service, and eventually break the All-Volunteer Force.[11]

This kind of firepower should end the argument, but Americans will have to let Congress know how they feel about sending their sons and daughters into a military that may one day harass them for their most deeply held beliefs. Chaplains will also have to search their souls as to whether they could serve in a military that would effectively bar them from honestly discussing biblical morality. The ACLU and the Anti-Defamation League have already demanded that the Naval Academy ban mealtime prayers (which the Navy has refused to do).[12]

As one of the most powerful transmitters of traditional values, the military has long been seen as an engine of social change. It's a captive audience of hundreds of thousands of men and women who will then go on to affect civilian life after leaving the service. This can be positive, as when the armed forces were racially integrated and helped speed the way for civil rights advances and the end of Jim Crow laws.

But the "progressive" strategy now is to hijack the moral capital of the civil rights movement and misapply it to promote sexual immorality and sexual confusion.

THE CAMPAIGN TO FEMINIZE G.I. JOE

With the advent of the feminist movement in the 1970s, the notion that the two sexes are interchangeable and that "gender" is merely in one's head—not one's biologically assigned sex—has collided with military culture.

Military historian Brian Mitchell has written extensively about the tie between the radical feminist agenda and the homosexual agenda for the military:

> The advocates of both share the same values, use the same arguments, and suffer from the same contradictions. Both would sacrifice national security to achieve ideological objectives. Both would use the military to provide radical social change. Both would have us believe that human sexuality is a purely private matter that ought not serve as a basis for public policy.[13]

After the Vietnam War, the number of women in the armed forces began to increase proportionally as gender roles became more fluid. Fewer men saw the military as a road to manhood, and more women were drawn to unconventional jobs. Over the years, many men have come to accept and welcome women into the military, as they have proved themselves to be capable, patriotic, and dedicated. Fraternization is still a major problem, however, and pregnancies and a higher incidence of injuries mean that women are more often discharged. In 2005, the Pentagon reported that between 1994 and 2003, a total of 26,446 women were discharged due to pregnancies.[14]

Over the years, more and more military positions were opened to women, since most of them did not depend on strength, endurance, or testosterone-driven male moxie. The exception is combat. Women are specifically exempted from combat duty for many reasons. First is the cultural imperative that men are supposed to protect women, not shove them into harm's way. Women were created by God to bear life, not take it—which is also why abortion is wrong.

Second, men are better suited for combat, being stronger, bigger, faster, and more aggressive. This is not simply opinion, but objective fact. Men and women are different. One sex is not "better" than the other, since both sexes have unique strengths and weaknesses. The radical feminist agenda ignores obvious truths in pursuit of a theoretical outcome. At present, women are being assigned to combat aircraft, but are still officially barred from ground combat.

In accommodating women at the nation's service academies, training has been softened, especially for strength and endurance. This emerged during the sworn testimony of a West Point official in 1991.[15]

Finally, the impact of women on men during combat is profound. The Israelis in 1948 first put women in the front lines, but withdrew them after seeing various problems, including men ignoring orders so they could protect female comrades.[16]

One of the more perverse developments from the feminist drive to put women in combat is an aspect of the military's Survival, Resistance, Evasion and Escape (SERE) program: they train men to be indifferent to women's screams. Kate O'Beirne, a member of the Presidential Commission on the Assignment of Women in the Armed Forces, sums up the barbaric nature of the campaign to desensitize men into relinquishing their protector's role:

> Good men protect and defend women in the face of a physical threat. If men in uniform are going to be expected to be sex blind when it comes to protecting their comrades, American mothers will have to get to work instructing their sons that it's okay to hit girls. Women have no "right" to serve in combat if their presence puts the men they serve with in jeopardy because these decent men are

determined to protect the weaker sex. Instructors at the military's SERE school for pilots saw that male students reacted more negatively to the simulated torture of female trainees and concluded that the men would have to be trained to inure themselves to the plight of women in pain.[17]

Perhaps the most comprehensive article of its kind, Elaine Donnelly's "Constructing the Co-Ed Military," in the *Duke Journal of Gender Law & Policy*[18] shows how the armed forces are gradually caving under feminist pressure to remove protections for women in the military. For example, the Army has a "co-location" rule, in which women are not to serve in units that would most likely come under enemy fire. The capture and subsequent sexual abuse of Lt. Jessica Lynch in Iraq in March 2003 showed why. Yet many women in Iraq and Afghanistan are in units that regularly come under fire, such as military police squads. Although some women apparently don't mind serving in combat, the overall effect of lifting the combat exemption could have enormous implications for all of society.

In the 1981 case, *Rostker v. Goldberg*,[19] the Supreme Court ruled that women are not subject to the draft because they do not serve in combat:

> [t]he existence of the combat restrictions clearly indicates the basis for Congress' decision to exempt women from registration. The purpose of registration was to prepare for a draft of combat troops. Since women are excluded from combat, Congress concluded that they would not be needed in the event of a draft, and therefore decided not to register them.[20]

If the military lifts the combat exemption, the United States could someday be drafting our daughters into the armed forces and into direct combat.

In his booklet *The Feminist Assault on the Military*, former Marxist ideologue David Horowitz, who became an outspoken conservative, relates how a leftwing professor claimed during the 1992 hearings before the Presidential Commission on the Assignment of Women in the Armed Forces that putting women in combat might help create "the idea that male fraternity and male respect of women was possible."[21] Horowitz marvels upon the feminist assumption that men think so little of women that it would take forcing them into combat to earn them any respect.

> Only a feminist ideologue could come up with such malicious lunacy. It only serves to confirm the suspicion that behind every radical feminist's concern for what women might be, lies a profound contempt for who they are.[22]

NINE

American Sovereignty
vs. the Global New Order

Since its founding, the United States has pursued a doctrine of American Exceptionalism. Many Americans believe they have been blessed by God with a unique set of circumstances allowing them to secure self-government, unparalleled freedom, and to avoid tyrannies common in much of the rest of the world.

In his incomparable 1831 study *Democracy in America*, Frenchman Alexis de Tocqueville wrote:

> The position of the Americans is therefore quite exceptional, and it may be believed that no democratic people will ever be placed in a similar one.

American presidents have voiced similar sentiments—that is, right up until the Obama administration.

Columnist Mark Steyn sums up the change in attitude this way:

> ... 100 days into a new presidency Barack Obama is giving strong signals to the world that we have entered what Caroline Glick of *The Jerusalem Post* calls "the post-American era." At the time of

[British Prime Minister] Gordon Brown's visit to Washington, London took umbrage at an Obama official's off-the-record sneer to a Fleet Street reporter that "there's nothing special about Britain. You're just the same as the other 190 countries in the world. You shouldn't expect special treatment." Andy McCarthy of *National Review* made the sharp observation that, never mind the British, this was how the administration felt about its own country, too: America is just the same as the other 190 countries in the world.

In Europe, the president was asked if he believed in "American exceptionalism," and he replied: "I believe in American exceptionalism, just as I suspect that the Brits believe in British exceptionalism and the Greeks believe in Greek exceptionalism."

Gee, thanks. A simple "no" would have sufficed. The president of the United States is telling us that American exceptionalism is no more than national chauvinism, a bit of flag-waving, of no more import than the Slovenes supporting the Slovene soccer team and the Papuans the Papuan soccer team.[1]

A corollary to America's unique founding is the patriotic notion that America will forge its own path in international matters, having fought a war to free itself from European domination.

This does not mean that the United States does not cooperate with other nations; we have signed treaties, fought two world wars, and intervened in others. It just means that America's leaders are duty bound to pursue the best interests of their nation, which may or may not be in accord with the views or interests of other nations.

In his Farewell Address, America's first president, George Washington, sharply warned Americans not to be tempted into overly constricting foreign alliances ...

> ... such attachments are particularly alarming to the truly enlightened and independent patriot. How many opportunities do they afford to tamper with domestic factions, to practice the arts of seduction, to mislead public opinion, to influence or awe the public councils! ... Against the insidious wiles of foreign influence (I conjure you to believe me fellow-citizens) the jealousy of a free people ought to be constantly awake, since history and experience prove that foreign influence is one of the most baneful foes of republican government.[2]

Washington was especially concerned about European powers:

> Our detached and distant situation invites and enables us to pursue a different course. ...Why forego the advantages of so peculiar a situation? Why quit our own to stand upon foreign ground? Why, by interweaving our destiny with that of any part of Europe, entangle our peace and prosperity in the toils of European ambition, rivalship, interest, humor or caprice?[3]

From the President on down, federal officials take an oath to uphold the Constitution of the United States. As Supreme Law of the Land, the Constitution trumps claims made by other nations to interfere in American law or commerce. The exception is treaties, which the Constitution specifically addresses in Article 6:

> This Constitution, and the Laws of the United States which shall be made in Pursuance thereof; and all Treaties made, or which shall be made, under the Authority of the United States, shall be the supreme Law of the Land; and the Judges in every State shall be bound thereby, any Thing in the Constitution or Laws of any State to the Contrary notwithstanding.

Because treaties have supreme legal authority, the United States has signed them infrequently and even reluctantly, except to ratify victories after winning wars.

Following World War II and facing a Cold War with communism, the U.S. joined the North Atlantic Treaty Organization (NATO) and other mutual defense pacts. Since 1945, with the establishment of the United Nations, there has been a sharp increase in the number of treaties[4] and international organizations.

The United States has signed some treaties, and pointedly declined to sign others.

In recent years, leftwing-dominated nations and America's home-grown "globalists" have campaigned to surrender great amounts of U.S. sovereignty under international auspices and for reasons having nothing to do with national security. Here are several of the more dangerous treaties that have gone unsigned, but are supported by the liberal leadership in the White House and Congress:

UNITED NATIONS CONVENTION ON THE RIGHTS OF THE CHILD

In November 1989, the United Nations General Assembly adopted the Convention on the Rights of the Child, with the treaty becoming operational on Sept. 2, 1990.[5]

The treaty "is the first legally binding international instrument to incorporate the full range of human rights—civil, cultural, economic, political and social rights," according to the UN.[6] The document's 54 chapters spell out the four core principles of the Convention: "non-discrimination; devotion to the best interests of the child; the right to life, survival and development; and respect for the views of the child."[7]

According to an analysis by Concerned Women for America, the Convention:

> ... usurps parental authority by embracing the view that children are autonomous agents who are capable, in all areas, of making adult decisions and dealing with adult situations. This radical legal doctrine stands in stark contrast to the traditional concept, upheld in America, that children are "minors" in need of parental protection.[8]

The treaty lists several "rights" that all children should have, regardless of parental concerns, such as the "right to freedom of expression; this right shall include freedom to seek, receive, and impart information and ideas of all kinds, regardless of frontiers, either orally, in writing or in print, in the form of art, or through any other media of the child's choice." (Article 13).

The United Nations Committee on the Rights of the Child has been campaigning since 1996 against spanking. In its "Violence Against Children in the Home and Family" report, the UN calls for a total ban on corporal punishment, regardless of parental values.[9]

In October 2003, a UN committee ruled that Canadian law allowing parents to spank their children violated the Rights of the Child convention and told Canada to scrap the law.[10]

Germany, which banned spanking in 2000, is now moving

toward a ban on home schooling. An anti-spanking group, Global Initiative to End All Corporal Punishment of Children, notes that Germany's spanking ban came about partly because of its adoption of the Convention on the Rights of the Child and because of a concerted public campaign:

> As long ago as 1980 the Civil Law was amended to give parents a duty to "discuss with the child questions relating to their care and upbringing and strive for a consensus." That this is completely unenforceable is not the point, since it creates an expectation that children have a legal right to be heard. It is possible that the attitudes brought about by the existence of this right for more than 20 years helped pave the way for the eventual ban on smacking.[11]

An American group, End Corporal Punishment in the Home Now, is calling for a ban on spanking in the United States, citing the UN:

> The UN Convention on the Rights of the Child through its Committee on the Rights of the Child has called on all member states to ban corporal punishment of children and institute education programs on positive discipline.[12]

In 2007, California Assemblywoman Sally J. Lieber introduced a bill prohibiting California's parents from spanking children younger than four years old, even in the home.[13] The bill was defeated amid a public outcry.

The campaign to end spanking, while often well meant, goes

directly against several of the Bible's admonitions to parents:

"Foolishness is bound up in the heart of a child; the rod of correction will drive it far from him." (Proverbs 22:15) "Do not withhold correction from a child, For if you beat him with a rod, he will not die. You shall beat him with a rod, and deliver his soul from hell." (Proverbs 23:13, 14)

CEDAW

Another positive-sounding treaty that could cost Americans their independence is the United Nations Convention on the Elimination of All Forms of Discrimination Against Women (CEDAW). President Carter signed it in 1980, but the Senate never ratified it.

Here's an analysis of the proposed treaty by Concerned Women for America (CWA):

CEDAW's definition of "discrimination" is all-encompassing and dangerous. It goes beyond trying to establish equality, which U.S. laws already afford women. CEDAW is actually a global Equal Rights Amendment, a tool for radical feminists, who deny any distinctions between men and women. CEDAW undermines the traditional family structure in the United States and other nations that respect the family. The preamble states, "A change in the traditional role of men as well as the role of women in society and in the family is needed to achieve full equality between men and women." Article 5a would require the United States government to "take all appropriate action" to:

"Modify the social and cultural patterns of
conduct of men and women, with a view
to achieving the elimination of prejudices
... based on ... stereotyped roles for men
and women."[14]

Nations that have already signed CEDAW have been subject
to intrusive reviews by United Nations bureaucrats. Here are a few
examples culled by CWA:

The CEDAW committee determines those
"stereotyped roles." For example, in its analysis of
Denmark, it "noted with concern that stereotypical
perceptions of gender role continued to exist in
society ... [that] kept men from assuming an equal
share of family responsibilities." In its 2000 review
of Belarus, the committee complained that
"Mothers' Day" and the "Mothers' Award"
encourage women's traditional roles. Also, the
CEDAW committee urged Armenia to "combat
the traditional stereotype of women in the noble role
of mother." Further, it complained to Luxembourg
about its "stereotypical attitudes that tend to portray
men as heads of households and breadwinners, and
women primarily as mothers and homemakers."[15]

CEDAW also promotes abortion, legalized prostitution, gender
re-education, homosexuality, government-mandated "comparable
worth," and encroaches on parental rights.[16]

LAW OF THE SEA

The Law of the Sea Treaty (LOST) could imperil America's leadership in undersea mineral mining, reducing incentives for exploration and transferring huge amounts of earned income to Third World nations. Doug Bandow, a senior fellow at the Cato Institute and former Special Assistant to President Ronald Reagan, explains in an American Spectator article how LOST would threaten American sovereignty:

> LOST, which essentially creates a second UN, is an artifact of the collectivist "New International Economic Order" popular in the 1970s, but is being resold as a guarantor of freedom of the seas.... LOST was originally promoted to redistribute wealth from First World democracies to Third World autocracies. The International Seabed Authority would regulate private ocean development, mine the seabed itself through an entity called "the Enterprise," and pay off favored nations and groups hither and yon.[17]

Bandow notes that academic proponents acknowledge that LOST could provide a framework for intrusive environmental demands, making it a "Trojan green horse."

> Professor William C.G. Burns of the Monterey Institute of International Studies wrote that the convention "may prove to be one of the primary battlegrounds for climate change issues in the future." In his view, "the potential impacts of rising sea surface temperatures, rising sea levels, and changes in ocean pH as a consequence of rising

levels of carbon dioxide in sea water" could "give rise to actions under the Convention's marine pollution provisions."

... The U.N.'s own Division for Ocean Affairs and the Law of the Sea proclaims that LOST is not "a static instrument, but rather a dynamic and evolving body of law that must be vigorously safeguarded and its implementation aggressively advanced."

If you like activist judges at the national level, imagine what you will get at the international level.

THE ENVIRONMENTAL GAMBIT

The largest threat looming to American independence is arguably the drive to put the nation under "green" treaties in the name of curbing "global warming" or "climate change." The largest item on the "green" agenda is to have the U.S. sign the Kyoto treaty, which implements anti-global warming goals created at the Earth Summit in Rio de Janeiro in 1992.

In 1997, the United Nations brokered the Kyoto Protocol, a treaty that requires industrialized nations to reduce "greenhouse gases" worldwide by 5.2 percent below 1990 levels, with 8 percent for the European Union and 7 percent for the United States.[18] Under the Clinton and Bush administrations, the treaty was not brought to the Senate for ratification. President Bush explicitly rejected the treaty in 2001, arguing that it would cripple industry, cost jobs, and ultimately prove ineffective in cleaning up the environment because of non-compliance by other nations such as India and China. In 2005, Bush told a Danish news agency that signing Kyoto would have "wrecked" the U.S. economy.[19]

Leaders of the 111th Congress and the Obama Administration are supporting the treaty, and are backing a "cap and trade" system in which industries would have to reduce carbon emissions or buy and trade credits. Administering such a system would be a nightmare, necessitating an enormous increase in government bureaucrats on the national and international levels with policing power. Both Barack Obama and John McCain back the creation of "cap and trade."

With liberals in charge of both houses of Congress and the White House, the usurpation of American sovereignty in the name of environmentalism has gone to a new level.

Epitomizing this trend is President Obama's nomination of former Yale Law School Dean Harold Koh to be the State Department's top lawyer. For years, Koh has lobbied for putting the United States under foreign authority. As former U.S. Sen. Rick Santorum writes, Koh has not been bashful about his aims:

> What is indisputable is that Koh calls himself a "transnationalist." He believes U.S. courts "must look beyond national interest to the mutual interests of all nations in a smoothly functioning international legal regime. ..." He thinks the courts have "a central role to play in domesticating international law into U.S. law" and should "use their interpretive powers to promote the development of a global legal system."[20]

SUBVERTING U.S. DOMESTIC LAW

Chillingly, several current and former justices of the U.S. Supreme Court agree that the U.S. should subsume its unique legal system under international standards.

In the landmark *Lawrence v. Texas*, in which the court in 2003 struck down state sodomy laws, Justice Anthony Kennedy, writing for the majority, cited flawed research from Great Britain and the

United Nations to back his view that sodomy was neither immoral nor unhealthy.[21]

In the Missouri juvenile death penalty case *Roper v. Simmons* (2005) Kennedy referred to the UN Convention on the Rights of the Child, amicus briefs from the European Union and Great Britain, and other international opinion in his majority opinion striking down a death sentence for a 17-year-old.

The killer, Charles Simmons, had told friends of wanting to kill someone and had assured them that he could "get away with it" because he was a juvenile. He and an accomplice broke into the home of Shirley Crook, with whom he had had an automobile collision, and the following took place, according to Kennedy's ruling:

> Using duct tape to cover her eyes and mouth and bind her hands, the two perpetrators put Mrs. Crook in her minivan and drove to a state park. They reinforced the bindings, covered her head with a towel, and walked her to a railroad trestle spanning the Meramec River. There they tied her hands and feet together with electrical wire, wrapped her whole face in duct tape and threw her from the bridge, drowning her in the waters below.
>
> By the afternoon of September 9, Steven Crook had returned home from an overnight trip, found his bedroom in disarray, and reported his wife missing.[22]

After the murder, Simmons continued to brag about the obviously pre-meditated killing.

The American Bar Assn., which has been controlled by liberals for many years, argued in the case that juveniles are not capable of the same moral judgments as adults:

Older adolescents behave differently than adults because their minds operate differently, their emotions are more volatile, and their brains are anatomically immature.[23]

As Justice Antonin Scalia pointed out in his dissent, the ABA's (and his colleagues') view of juvenile fallibility in this criminal case contrasts sharply with other rulings that claimed juvenile competence when it came to safeguarding minor girls from being subjected to abortions without their parents' consent or knowledge.

Scalia also criticized his colleagues for bowing to foreign opinion:

The Court thus proclaims itself sole arbiter of our Nation's moral standards, and in the course of discharging that awesome responsibility purports to take guidance from the views of foreign courts and legislatures. Because I do not believe that the meaning of our Eighth Amendment, any more than the meaning of other provisions of our Constitution, should be determined by the subjective views of five Members of this Court and like-minded foreigners, I dissent.[24]

In speeches before civic groups, Kennedy, Stephen Breyer, Ruth Bader Ginsburg and former Justice Sandra Day O'Connor all have argued that U.S. courts should incorporate foreign law and foreign court decisions, even if it means overriding laws passed by duly elected American lawmakers.

On April 10, 2009, Ginsburg vigorously defended the use of foreign sources during a speech at a symposium at Ohio State, where she complained that the Canadian Supreme Court is cited more often internationally than the U.S. high court.[25]

Former Justice Sandra Day O'Connor put it this way at an awards dinner in 2003:

> I suspect that over time we will rely increasingly, or take notice at least increasingly, on international and foreign courts in examining domestic issues ... [this] may not only enrich our own country's decisions, I think it may create that all important good impression.[26]

Santorum writes that such over-weaning deference to other nations' legal trends violates the essence of American independence:

> ... "[T]ransnationalism" stands in contrast to good, old-fashioned notions of national sovereignty, in which our Constitution is the highest law of the land. In the traditional view, controversial matters, whatever they may be, are subject to democratic debate here. They should be resolved by the American people and their representatives, not "internationalized." What Holland or Belgium or Kenya or any other nation or coalition of nations thinks has no bearing on our exercise of executive, legislative, or judicial power.[27]

America is in danger of losing its sovereignty when elected officials, judges, and bureaucrats cede moral and legal authority to foreign influence, treaties, and international organizations.

If America is, as President Obama appears to believe, just one among 180 nations, no better or worse, and with no unique heritage worth defending, it becomes easier to just go along with the crowd toward a Global New Order.

For Christians and others who march to the beat of a different drummer, and who have unparalleled constitutionally guaranteed freedoms in the U.S., it could mean serious erosion of long-assumed protections.

TEN

Freedom of Speech, for Some

In recent years, there have been numerous attempts—many successful—to censor people and viewpoints that oppose liberalism.

In public schools, and even some private schools, students have been told that any open support of traditional morality is a form of bigotry toward homosexuals, transgenders, or other non-conventional "sexual minorities."

Use of terms that reflect the nation's Christian heritage and current Christian majority, such as Christmas and Easter, have been banned and replaced with Winter Break and Spring Break. Christmas carols, long a staple of school music programs in December, are disappearing, replaced by "safe" secular songs such as *Frosty the Snowman.*

On college campuses, "speech codes" have arisen that translate conservative opinion into "hate speech" that campuses can and do ban. Authorities are still taking their cue from Marxist scholar Herbert Marcuse, who during the 1960s helped transform universities into Petri dishes of radical activism that would not tolerate dissent. In fact, in his influential 1965 essay "Repressive Tolerance," Marcuse openly proclaimed that campus revolutionaries should silence "oppressive" conservatives and be "intolerant towards the protagonists of the repressive status quo."[1] More specifically, he writes:

"... [W]here freedom and happiness themselves are at stake ... certain things cannot be said, certain ideas cannot be expressed, certain policies cannot be proposed, certain behavior cannot be permitted without making tolerance an instrument for the continuation of servitude."[2]

One example of this kind of treatment was noted by columnist Don Feder:

At Ohio State University's Mansfield campus in 2006, the entire faculty voted to file charges of sexual discrimination and harassment against librarian Scott Savage for recommending three conservative books to incoming freshmen.[3]

Speaking of Mr. Feder, he has had his own brushes with radicals. An Orthodox Jew, Feder was shouted down at the University of Massachusetts in March 2009.[4] On his Web site, Feder, a former *Boston Herald* columnist and now a political consultant, describes his views this way:

I believe in God, America and the family ... I believe in Biblical morality, often designated Judeo-Christian ethics.... any attempt to separate America from God is a betrayal of our Republic.[5]

This kind of stuff was too much for the students at U. Mass, who wrecked the March 10 event. Here's how Feder describes the scene:

The [students] unfurled banners, waved signs, chanted slogans, shouted insults and taunts, jeered, laughed derisively, and generally demonstrated the self-control of toddlers with Tourette's syndrome. Their signs read, "Hate Speech Leads to Hate Crimes" (this from people who insist there's no connection between pornography and sex crimes), "Free Speech Does Not Equal Hate Speech" (who decides what speech should be censored in the name of countering hatred? They do, of course) and—my favorite—"Abolish Hate." Bravo! After that, we can abolish lust, greed, sloth and unhygienic habits (though the protestors might consider that a personal attack). My terrier has taken to toting around a sign that says "Abolish Cats!"[6]

At the University of North Carolina (UNC), former Rep. Tom Tancredo (R-Col.), a foe of illegal immigration, was driven from the podium on April 14, 2009, by students who jeered and blocked him with a banner.[7] A week later, on April 22, former Rep. Virgil Goode (R-Va.), who opposes racial affirmative action, was heckled at UNC and interrupted with electronic devices.[8] To their credit, UNC administrators condemned these attacks on free speech, and pledged to prevent further such incidents. But no action was taken against the perpetrators.

Contrast that with the treatment of two pro-life, conservative students from Claremont McKenna College in California, who attended a lecture on February 19, 2009, by a Planned Parenthood representative at Pomona College. The students asked questions and videotaped the responses, but turned off the camera when asked. Nonetheless, two deans charged the students with "harassment or hostile behavior" and had them banned from the Pomona campus. After Claremont faculty and alumni complained, Pomona lifted the ban.[9]

In 2008, pro-family conservative writer Ryan Sorba faced down a hostile screaming crowd of lesbians at Smith College, but finally had to give up his speech about the history and realities of the homosexual agenda.[10]

HATE CRIMES LAW IS ENACTED

On October 28, 2009, President Obama signed the Matthew Shepard and James Byrd Jr. Hate Crimes Prevention Act of 2009 as part of the National Defense Authorization Act for 2010 (H.R. 2647).[11] Although the law says that additional penalties will be added to criminal sentences only involving violent acts, the federal "hate crimes" bill is a centerpiece of homosexual activists' strategy to reshape society.

Beyond the unfairness of excluding some groups, such as the homeless and children, the law advances an underlying ambitious agenda to punish individuals and groups that hold traditional values.

During the Supreme Court hearings on the Boy Scouts case (Boy Scouts of America vs. Dale, 2000), the Rev. Rob Schenck of the National Clergy Council was sitting next to the White House liaison on gay and lesbian issues. Thinking he was of like mind, she whispered to him:

"We're not going to win this case, but that's okay. Once we get 'hate crime' laws on the books, we're going to go after the Scouts and all the other bigots."[12]

The hate crimes law adds "sexual orientation" and "gender identity" to a list of specially protected classes such as race, ethnicity, sex and religion. Congress thus created newly minted "civil rights" based on sexual vagaries. Like "sexual orientation," "gender identity" is fluid, and it includes transvestitism (cross-dressing) and transsexualism. It is notable that former homosexuals, or "ex-gays," perhaps the most victimized group based on "sexual orientation" perceptions, were not mentioned as being covered by this bill. In the

House, even an amendment to exclude "pedophilia" was defeated.

In 2008, America had more than 11 million incidents of violence or property crime,[13] of which 7,783 incidents were classified as "hate crimes, of which 1,297 involved "sexual orientation."[14] Not exactly an epidemic of "hate" in a nation of more than 310 million.

Despite assurances that the law targets only violent acts—which are already illegal—the law essentially criminalizes views or beliefs because defendants' speech, writing, reading materials and organizational memberships will become key evidence to establish a "hate crime."

The tendency to equate conservative views with "extremism" was on display in 2009 when a revealing memo surfaced at the Department of Homeland Security, for which Secretary Janet Napolitano was forced to apologize. The memo, "Rightwing Extremism: Current Economic and Political Climate Fueling Resurgence in Radicalization and Recruitment,"[15] listed as candidates for "violent radicalization" such Americans as returning veterans from the Iraq and Afghanistan wars, people who oppose illegal immigration, abortion, and gun control, and those who warn of losing American sovereignty to globalism. This characterization of millions of Americans as security threats should give everyone pause about passing laws that redefine legal protection based on group status.

The federal hate crime law will politicize crime, leading to pressure on police and prosecutors to devote more of their limited resources to some victims over others.

Hate crime laws lay the groundwork for assaults on freedom of speech and freedom of religion. We can look to our northern neighbor for clues about what happens when such laws are enacted. In Saskatchewan, Canada, a newspaper publisher and a man who placed a newspaper ad faced jail and were fined $4,500 each, merely for running an ad containing references to several Bible verses regarding homosexuality.[16] A college teacher who wrote a letter to the editor affirming traditional morality was suspended.[17] And best-selling author Mark Steyn (*America Alone*), faced charges in national and provincial tribunals for the supposed "hate crime" of reporting what Muslim leaders in Europe themselves say about changing demographics.[18]

USING INTIMIDATION TO SILENCE OPPONENTS

Since the 1960s, the Left has engaged in a campaign called the "politics of personal destruction." They have lost the war of ideas, so they have resorted to two essential tactics: disruption and *ad hominem* attacks on people's character. They simply will not allow the truth to be told if they can help it.

The jackboot tactics have not been confined to campuses. Churches that have dared challenge homosexuality have also come in for disruptive demonstrations. For example:

On April 26, 2009, homosexual activists invaded the grounds of a Boston church, trampled a graveyard, and placed bullhorns up against the windows, trying to terrify those inside. The reason? The Park Street Church was hosting a presentation by Exodus International about people overcoming homosexuality through the grace of Jesus Christ. "Massresistance," a pro-family group, videotaped the mob scene and posted it on their Web site.[19]

Finally, even many liberals were taken aback by the abuse of Miss California, Carrie Prejean, at the 2009 Miss USA pageant on April 19. A flamboyant homosexual blogger who calls himself Perez Hilton, and who inexplicably was a judge at the event, asked Miss Prejean what she thought about Vermont legalizing same-sex "marriage." When she responded with her personal view that marriage was the union of a man and a woman, Hilton scowled. Immediately afterward, he boasted that he gave her a "zero," costing her the title, and denounced her in a video on his blog—using foul language. The next morning, he did the same during an MSNBC interview.

And what did pageant officials do in light of this horrible abuse of a contestant for voicing an opinion held by a majority of Americans? They sided with Hilton and lamented Prejean's lack of "tolerance." Donald Trump, the pageant's main sponsor, also did nothing to discipline either Hilton or the pageant officials, who cheered his disgusting behavior.

The message was clear: if you disagree with any aspect of the homosexual cultural and political agenda in public, you will be persecuted.

The silver lining is that many Americans who had been indifferent or even supportive of the homosexual agenda got a wake-up call about what it will be like for everyone if this movement and the rest of the radical Left succeed in crushing dissent.

THE WAR ON POLITICAL FREE SPEECH

In March 2002, Congress passed, and President George W. Bush signed, the Bipartisan Campaign Reform Act, which greatly restricted spending by corporations and unions just prior to elections.[20] On Jan. 21, 2010, the U.S. Supreme Court struck down what became known as the McCain-Feingold Act.[21] It was a major victory for freedom of speech and holding incumbents accountable. In *Citizens United v. FEC*,[22] the court not only overturned most of the restrictions but also a previous ruling regarding campaign financing. The case was brought by Citizens United, a conservative group that wanted to air a 90-minute documentary critical of Hillary Clinton during her presidential primary run in 2008. The court ruled that preventing the group from airing the film amounted to unconstitutional censorship.

In response, Democrats immediately introduced the Democracy Is Strengthened by Casting Light on Spending in Elections Act[23] (DISCLOSE ACT), which would severely restrict corporations and nonprofits but leave unions to spend freely. The DISCLOSE Act was a naked attempt to strangle conservative opposition before the 2010 and 2012 elections. On June 24, 2010, the House passed the DISCLOSE Act.[24] On July 27, 2010, however, the Senate in a party-line, 41 to 57, vote rejected cloture on a GOP filibuster of the bill.[25] Chief sponsor Sen. Charles Schumer (D-New York) vowed to bring it back again and again until it passed.

The importance of the Supreme Court's affirmation of groups' freedom of speech cannot be understated. Without such freedom to purchase ads, the vast amount of information about candidates is available mainly through media coverage, which is almost uniformly liberal.

Ironically, the regained freedom to advertise that was condemned by liberal editorial writers probably was greeted with a cheer by the same media's business managers, since they stand to gain substantially from ad purchases.

But the legal war over this exposes the fragility of freedom of speech. Without the Supreme Court's reassertion of the First Amendment, secular socialists might feel empowered to try to stop distribution of anything reflecting badly on them at election time.

THE RETURN OF THE FAIRNESS DOCTRINE

On a national level, the Left is threatening to revive the so-called Fairness Doctrine, a Federal Communications Commission policy that was in effect from 1949 to 1987, and which effectively squelched the airing of political opinions on the radio.

Stations avoided discussing issues of substance to avoid bureaucratic interference and red tape, and ceding valuable airtime to liberal voices that few wanted to hear. But during the 1990s, without the Fairness Doctrine to hold them back, conservative and Christian talk radio took off, led by Rush Limbaugh and Christian programs such as Coral Ridge's *Truths That Transform* with

Dr. D. James Kennedy.

As liberals failed to sustain competitive programs on the radio airwaves, "progressives" such as Sens. Chuck Schumer (D-N.Y.) and Dianne Feinstein (D-Calif.) began talking about ways to silence their opponents.

On February 12, 2009, former President Bill Clinton said on a liberal talk show that America needs the Fairness Doctrine, because conservative talk radio is sounding "a blatant drumbeat" against the Obama Administration's stimulus package. He complained that "there has always been a lot of big money to support the right-wing talk shows."

Well, there's big money because millions tune in to those shows. Sponsors support programs that people want.

Clinton's call for government-enforced intrusion into the airwaves came days after similar remarks by Sens. Tom Harkin (D-Iowa) and Debbie Stabenow (D-Mich.). The growing liberal affection for the idea of reining in talk radio should send a chill up any freedom lover's back.

During the Cold War, people in the Eastern Bloc literally risked their lives to listen to Radio Free Europe. Even if local broadcasters had aired unfiltered news, the people had no freedom to listen and faced arrest. Freedom of speech without the freedom to listen is useless. Although a renewed Fairness Doctrine would not send government goons to people's doors, it would cast a chill on freedom of speech and the freedom to listen.

On February 26, 2009, the U.S. Senate passed by an 87 to 11 vote an amendment to the District of Columbia Voting Rights Act that would bar the FCC from reviving the Fairness Doctrine. Sponsored by Sen. Jim DeMint (R-South Carolina), the Broadcaster Freedom Act was countered the same day in the same bill with an amendment by Sen. Richard J. Durbin (D-Illinois) that requires the FCC to promote "diversity" in ownership and restates the FCC's right to renew licenses based on whether stations "operate in the public interest."

"Sen. Durbin's amendment exposed the Democrat intentions to impose radio censorship through the back door, using vague regulations dealing with media ownership," Sen. DeMint said.[26]

On the surface, the Fairness Doctrine sounds like a good idea. Why not ensure that differing viewpoints are aired? This might have made sense at one time. But the Internet, cable TV, and the radio renaissance have given Americans literally thousands of choices. Besides, the federal taxpayer already subsidizes 860 National Public Radio stations with an estimated weekly audience of 23 million. Three other noncommercial liberal networks—Pacifica Radio, American Public Media and Public Radio International, collectively have 31 news/talk shows on the radio and Internet.

If the FCC forces stations to carry a response each time Rush Limbaugh offers an opinion, this would create unsponsored airtime. During the Fairness Doctrine era from 1949 to 1987, many stations skipped political talk. The Fairness Doctrine, which should be titled the Censorship Doctrine, would effectively end conservative and Christian radio discussion, leaving a liberal monopoly. Would a Christian station, for example, have to carry speeches from a local Muslim or Buddhist? Many would shut down before being used in such a way.

The Fairness Doctrine is not only dangerous, but utterly unnecessary when it comes to guaranteeing a variety of media information and viewpoints.

A 2008 report by the Culture and Media Institute, "Unmasking the Myths Behind the Fairness Doctrine," provides striking evidence that liberals dominate all but talk radio:

- Broadcast TV news (liberal, 42.1 million daily viewers vs. 0 conservative)

- Top 25 newspapers (liberal 11.7 million circulation vs. 1.3 million conservative)
- Cable TV news (liberal 182.8 viewers per month vs. 61.6 million conservative)
- Major newsweeklies (liberal 8.5 million weekly circulation vs. 0 conservative)[27]

Conservative talk radio has an estimated weekly audience of 87 million listeners vs. liberal programs reaching 24.5 million. The top 13 talk shows are all hosted by conservatives such as Limbaugh, Sean Hannity, Michael Savage, Glenn Beck, Laura Ingraham and Mark Levin. Only four liberal talk show hosts even crack the top 20: Ed Schultz (14) Alan Colmes (17), Thom Hartmann (18) and Lionel (20).[28] Liberal radio network Air America is on life support.

Fox News Channel dominates cable TV news, with only CNN's *Larry King Live* cracking the top five. But Fox News Channel's top-rated *The O'Reilly Factor* has less than half the viewers (2.6 million) of the lowest-rated network news show, *CBS Evening News*, which averaged 6.1 million viewers in 2008.[29]

Despite the overwhelming liberal media advantage, conservatives and Christians are not calling for a Fairness Doctrine for newspapers, or broadcast news or magazines. In fact, conservatives and Christians welcome liberals to the free-wheeling world of talk radio, but as competitors, not usurpers. It's one thing to work hard to attract a market. It's another to install unwanted voices at government gunpoint.

THE NEW GAME PLAN TO "FIX" TALK RADIO

Knowing that many Americans are alerted to the dangers posed by the Fairness Doctrine, liberals are poised to bring it about through the back door, by creating "community monitoring boards," "localism" requirements and changing licensing rules. Imagine an ACORN-dominated "community board" presenting evidence at a station's licensing renewal that there was not enough "diversity" in programming.

On July 29, 2009, Obama appointed Mark Lloyd as Associate General Counsel and Chief Diversity Officer (informally known as "the diversity czar") at the Federal Communications Commission (FCC). The FCC regulates broadcast radio and television and is beginning to regulate the Internet. Putting Lloyd in this post is putting the fox in charge of the henhouse.

As a Senior Fellow at the leftwing Center for American Progress (CAP), Lloyd co-wrote a June 2007 report with authors from another leftwing group, the Free Press, entitled "The Structural Imbalance of Political Talk Radio."[30] The Free Press was co-founded by avowed Marxist Robert McChesney and had fellow communist Van Jones on its board until he resigned in 2008. As Accuracy in Media reports: "In an article in the socialist Monthly Review, 'Journalism, Democracy, and Class Struggle,' Chesney declared, 'Our job is to make media reform part of our broader struggle for democracy, social justice, and, dare we say it, socialism.'[31] McChesney introduced Obama's former pastor, Jeremiah Wright, at an anniversary celebration of the Review on Sept. 17, 2009.[32] Wright praised the Review's "no-nonsense Marxism."[33]

Lloyd's book and the CAP report argue for forcing private broadcasters to heavily subsidize public broadcasting.[34] Lloyd essentially sees conservative talk radio as a menace and is well positioned to undercut its influence. The FCC is also moving toward regulating content on the Internet, a topic I address in *How Liberals Are Trying to Shut Down Media Freedom in the U.S.*, available at coralridge.org.

The American people still have a constitutional guarantee of freedom of speech. But it will become much less meaningful if a revived Fairness Doctrine or its equivalent deprives them of the freedom to listen.

ELEVEN

Health Care:
Reform or Rationing?

*"We have to pass this bill so the
American people can find out what's in it."*
House Speaker Nancy Pelosi

*"We consider health reform to have been an important battle
and a success of his (Obama's) government."*
Cuban dictator Fidel Castro,
*who called passage of America's government
takeover of health care a "miracle."*[1]

After strong-arm tactics and a monumental debate that tied up Congress for nearly a year, President Obama signed on March 23, 2010, a law that amounts to a federal government takeover of the nation's health care system. The good news is that it tied up the activist Congress so that it could not pass other dangerous bills. The bad news is that this law is about as dangerous as it gets.

Despite a steadily rising majority of Americans opposing the bill, Senate leaders had used several parliamentary maneuvers to pass it on Christmas Eve. On March 25, by a vote of 56 to 43, the Senate passed a "reconciliation" bill that was supposed to address some House members' concerns, after which the House passed the Senate bill again, 220 to 207.

The linchpin for passage was the decision of Rep. Bart Stupak (D-Mich.), leader of the "pro-life Democrats," to vote for the bill despite warnings that it would mandate taxpayer funding of abortion. Stupak agreed after President Obama signed an executive order (which is far weaker than an actual law and can be undone at the stroke of a pen) restricting taxpayer funding of abortion. The ploy worked, resistance collapsed, and the bill narrowly passed.

The debate spawned not only the emergence of the nationwide Tea Party movement but numerous pledges by office holders to repeal the law. If they don't, this law could spell the end of freedom as we know it. Twenty-one states have joined in lawsuits claiming that the law is unconstitutional because it includes an individual mandate to purchase health insurance.[2]

The final bill is about 2,700 pages long. Despite Mrs. Pelosi's assurance, no one is sure about what is in the bill. It is profoundly complex. Before its passage, President Obama argued vehemently that the individual insurance mandate is "absolutely not a tax increase." But his Justice Department announced in July 2010 that it would defend the new law as an exercise of Congress's power to "lay and collect taxes."

As the American Civil Rights Union's Senior Fellow J. Kenneth Blackwell and Senior Legal Analyst Ken Klukowski argued in a July 22, 2010 *Wall Street Journal* article, Obama was right—the Constitution gives Congress no power to regard a purchasing mandate as a "tax."[3] Why, then, would Obama's own Attorney General turn around and try to use the tax claim to defend the law? Well, because the Constitution gives Congress no power to force Americans to purchase a product, either. As for the change in strategy in defending the law, no one could accuse the Obama

Administration from over indulging in consistency when it comes to justifying policy initiatives. The only real consistency is its relentless drive to increase government power and spending.

Dropping another shoe in the Administration's quest to turn America's health care system into one resembling the socialist systems in Cuba and Great Britain, Obama in July 2010 appointed Donald Berwick of Harvard to direct the Centers for Medicare and Medicaid Services. An unabashed admirer of what he calls Cuba's health care "miracle," Berwick also has warned of "the darkness of private enterprise." He said that "excellent health care is by definition redistributionist," and that he has a "love" for Britain's National Health Service.[4] Have we mentioned that Britain's system has what amounts to "death panels" that deny care to patients that are deemed not worth the expense?

It's no wonder that Obama bypassed Senate confirmation and placed Berwick via a recess appointment. He's managing an $800 billion system, and the senators might have had some questions about where he would like to take it.

As for the rest of ObamaCare, most of which takes effect in 2014, here is some of the immediate fallout:

The law reduces the tax break that corporations receive for offering health benefit plans to their employees. Columnist Mark Steyn explains what this did:

> On the day President Obama signed Obamacare into law, Verizon sent an e-mail to all its employees warning that the company's costs "will increase in the short term." And in the medium term? Well, U.S. corporations that are able to do so will get out of their prescription drug plans and toss their retirees onto the Medicare pile. So far, just three companies—John Deere & Co., Caterpillar and

Valero Energy Corp.—have calculated that the loss of the deduction will add a combined $265 million to their costs."[5]

AT&T announced that it would have to take a $1 billion write down as a direct result of Obamacare. And after several other companies warned stockholders of the possibility of increased costs and thus a decrease in profits—a duty they had to perform or risk penalties under federal accounting law—liberal congressmen including Rep. Henry Waxman (D.-Calif.) and Stupak summoned them to a hearing on April 21 to threaten them.[6]

More fallout is in store because estimates of government costs for big programs like health care have invariably been ridiculously short of actual costs. ObamaCare, according to White House Senior Advisor David Axelrod, was based on "the template" of the Massachusetts system launched under Republican Gov. Mitt Romney. That program, which includes an individual mandate, has become a nightmare for Bay State taxpayers. Massachusetts Treasurer Timothy Cahill summarized the problem in an article:

> As state treasurer, I can speak with authority about the Massachusetts pilot program. It has been a fiscal train wreck.
>
> The universal insurance coverage we adopted in 2006 was projected to cost taxpayers $88 million a year. However, since this program was adopted in 2006, our health-care costs have in total exceeded $4 billion.[7]

Tucked into the monstrous ObamaCare law are budget gimmicks that will quickly come undone as the system expands exponentially.

After taking out the "public option" to ensure victory, liberal

Democrats moved almost immediately to put it back, introducing in July 2010 a bill, the Public Option Act (HR 5808). This "public option" insurance coverage[8] would doom private insurance and was a major factor in holding up the overall bill. The lead sponsor is Pete Stark, the California atheist who has worked hard over the years to turn America into a secular, socialist nation. You can't say that the liberals are shy about grabbing every last bit of power that they can, while they can.

Mark Steyn, noting the effect that nationalized health care has had on European countries, sums up why Obama and his party were willing even to lose big in the mid-term 2010 elections and beyond to establish a government-run health system:

> The governmentalization of health care is the fastest way to a permanent left-of-center political culture. It redefines the relationship between the citizen and the state in fundamental ways that make limited government all but impossible.... The result is a kind of two-party one-party state: Right-of-center parties will once in a while be in office, but never in power, merely presiding over vast left-wing bureaucracies that cruise on regardless.[9]

Andrew McCarthy, another insightful political analyst, warns:

> Health care is a loser for the Left only if the Right has the steel to undo it. The Left is banking on an absence of steel.[10]

The Patient Protection and Affordable Care Act[11] of 2010 contains so many intrusive, expensive and dangerous aspects, that it needs repeal, not tinkering. Here are just a few, as reported verbatim from a March 11, 2010 letter from the Congressional Budget Office to Sen. Harry Reid:

The legislation will:

- Establish a mandate for most residents of the United States to obtain health insurance.
- Set up insurance exchanges through which certain individuals and families could receive federal subsidies to substantially reduce the cost of purchasing that coverage.
- Significantly expand eligibility for Medicaid.
- Substantially reduce the growth of Medicare's payment rates for most services (relative to the growth rates projected under current law).
- Impose an excise tax on insurance plans with relatively high premiums.
- Make various other changes to the federal tax code, Medicare, Medicaid, and other programs.[12]

The CBO, whose director was summoned to the White House in 2009 after the CBO released figures showing the health care law would cost more than its supporters originally claimed, also says in this letter that the law will create "a net reduction in federal deficits of $118 billion over the 2010–2019 period." That would be a first for the federal government. Costs for Medicare, Medicaid, food stamps and other federal programs have risen exponentially past their original estimates, going from millions to billions very quickly.

Here's a far less rosy view of the fiscal and social consequences of the new law, courtesy of Michael Tanner of the libertarian Cato Institute:

- While the new law will increase the number

of Americans with insurance coverage, it falls significantly short of universal coverage. By 2019, roughly 21 million Americans will still be uninsured.

- The legislation will cost far more than advertised, more than $2.7 trillion over 10 years of full implementation, and will add $352 billion to the national debt over that period.

- Most American workers and businesses will see little or no change in their skyrocketing insurance costs, while millions of others, including younger and healthier workers and those who buy insurance on their own through the non-group market will actually see their premiums go up faster as a result of this legislation.

- The new law will increase taxes by more than $669 billion between now and 2019, and the burdens it places on business will significantly reduce economic growth and employment.

- While the law contains few direct provisions for rationing care, it nonetheless sets the stage for government rationing and interference with how doctors practice medicine.

- Millions of Americans who are happy with their current health insurance will not be able to keep it.[13]

Another troubling aspect of the law is that the Internal Revenue Service will take on vast new powers. The agency has asked to hire hundreds of employees to assist in compliance, and even the liberal-leaning FactCheck estimates that it could take 5,000 new IRS employees (some critics of the law estimate as many as 16,500 new employees will be needed).[14]

Starting in 2012, all businesses and tax-exempt organizations must issue an IRS form called a 1099 to vendors from whom they purchase goods totaling $600 or more annually. That's right. It will take only $600 to create more paperwork for even small, independent businesses. As *The Washington Post* observes, "it will demand thorough record-keeping on the part of buyers."[15]

THE LONG-TERM STRATEGY

After First Lady Hillary Clinton's sweeping attempt to take over the health-care industry failed in the mid-1990s, "progressives" have discussed ways to do the same thing without upsetting the public. The Left wants to control health care so that the government would assume literally the power of life and death over America's families. Just the threat of withholding medical care is enough for many people to surrender other freedoms to the government. Such a system also reinforces the idea that government is God.

The liberal rhetoric has remained the same: "The health-care system is broken;" America "is facing a health-care crisis." And so on. Never mind that America's health-care system is the envy of the world and is far and away the world's leader in innovation. America develops more new drugs than any other country and more new treatments. And whenever a health crisis hits another country, America's unparalleled system springs into action to help.

Health-care reform is needed to see that more people are insured and to reduce bloated costs, but the best solutions involve less government, not more. Several plans propose creating tax incentives for people to decide how much insurance to purchase on their own and to keep control over their own medical decisions. But these proposals are given short shrift in most media, which remain infatuated with the massive government expansion into the health-care field.

It's not as if we don't have abundant examples of where this will lead if not repealed. In countries where the government has laid a heavy hand on medicine, as in Great Britain, innovation has been stifled. Patients face long waits for routine surgeries, and bureaucrats decide who gets certain treatments. The Institute of Economic Affairs in London published a book in 2000 that included these observations:

> Of course, UK health care is cheap. We spend less on health care than does any comparable nation, but the cheapness of the NHS is subsidised by the exhaustion and demoralisation of the staff and by the second-rate service it so often provides. It is the cheapness of the miser who knows the price of everything and the value of nothing. And it is a cheapness that demeans patients as supplicants and which hides the medical realities of rationing from them.[16]

The report examines some of the more dangerous realities facing patients with serious conditions:

> Often treatment is not withheld altogether, but it is *delayed*, sometimes with the result that the patient's condition worsens. There are measures of delay, not least the waiting lists, although their impact on outcomes is not always clear cut. *The National Survey of NHS Patients*, published by the Department of Health, is also a useful guide. It found that one in ten patients were seen by a specialist on the same day as they were referred by their GP. About 50 per cent had to wait over a month and 20 per cent more than three months.

Over one in three of those waiting said that their condition had got worse while they were waiting and 14 per cent claimed to be "in a lot of pain."[17]

The Obama Administration and its allies in Congress are still carefully avoiding talk of the government health care "takeover," but their new law does exactly that. And the net result will not be better care, but rationing of health care by government bureaucrats.

The initial tact was that creation of a new government health insurance program would ostensibly be available to everyone.[18] Private health insurance, we are told, will still be offered. But the playing field will tip severely to the left, with the government's enormous competitive advantages. Businesses and individuals will be tempted to abandon private care and take a ride on the government's ambulance. When enough of them do so, the private system will collapse, and the government will take over with a single-payer system. This will effectively end choice for consumers and give bureaucrats tremendous power.

Doctors are already in great numbers refusing to take Medicare and Medicaid payments, because filling out red tape for the relatively small payments is not worth it. In a column for the *Wall Street Journal*, Dr. Marc Siegel, who practices medicine in New York, warns that further government encroachment on medicine will not make it any better:

> Bottom line: None of the current plans, government or private, provide my patients with the care they need. And the care that is provided is increasingly expensive and requires a big battle for approvals. Of course, we're promised by the Obama administration that universal health insurance will avoid all these problems. But how is that possible

when you consider that the medical turnstiles will be the same as they are now, only they will be clogged with more and more patients? The doctors that remain in this expanded system will be even more overwhelmed than we are now.

I wouldn't want to be a patient when that happens.[19]

The temptation will be strong to shift the focus from the best care to what is most economical. The argument will be that since there is only so much health care money to go around, that the most productive people should receive it. Since older people need far more medical care, including prescriptions, than young people, bureaucrats will begin denying them services. The infirm, the aged, and unborn babies with defects will be the first to bear the brunt of the "savings."

DISPLACING PRIVATE INSURANCE

The scariest part is that most people believe that they will be able to obtain private care in such a system if they are still willing to pay for it. But the reality is that once the government single-payer system is in place, no amount of money will buy a treatment if a bureaucrat does not think you deserve it.

In an interview with *The New York Times*, President Obama was asked about dealing with higher medical care costs for the aged.[20] The answer came just after Obama described his own family's dilemma when his grandmother needed a hip replacement, but was dying of cancer. Here is part of the transcript:

> **THE PRESIDENT:** So that's where I think you just get into some very difficult moral issues. But that's also a huge driver of cost, right? I mean, the

chronically ill and those toward the end of their lives are accounting for potentially 80 percent of the total health care bill out here.

So how do you—how do we deal with it?

THE PRESIDENT: Well, I think that there is going to have to be a conversation that is guided by doctors, scientists, ethicists. And then there is going to have to be a very difficult democratic conversation that takes place. It is very difficult to imagine the country making those decisions just through the normal political channels. And that's part of why you have to have some independent group that can give you guidance. It's not determinative, but I think has to be able to give you some guidance. And that's part of what I suspect you'll see emerging out of the various health care conversations that are taking place on the Hill right now.

A *Washington Times* editorial that analyzed the president's remarks said this:

It's a scary picture the president paints.... The time to really worry about your health is when a government bureaucrat, not your personal doctor, tells you what treatment you can have. Yet that's exactly the scenario endorsed by Mr. Obama. This position clearly leads to health care rationing. Nobody in the government or in any "political channels" should tell individuals how to make decisions about "the end of their lives." The only conversations happening should be personal, not democratic. It's not up to government to pull the plug.[21]

A picture of such a future is already available in Oregon, where some patients have been told that because chemotherapy will extend their lives only so long, the state-run medical system will instead offer to pay only for helping them to commit suicide.[22]

Randy Stroup, 53, a cancer patient, applied for aid under the state's Oregon Health Plan in 2008, and received a letter saying that he would get no money for chemotherapy, but could get money to help him kill himself.[23] He finally received aid for chemo after fighting the system.

Fox News explains:

> Oregon doesn't cover life-prolonging treatment unless there is better than a 5 percent chance it will help the patients live for five more years—but it covers doctor-assisted suicide, defining it as a means of providing comfort, no different from hospice care or pain medication.
>
> "It's chilling when you think about it," said Dr. William Toffler, a professor of family medicine at Oregon Health & Science University. "It absolutely conveys to the patient that continued living isn't worthwhile."[24]

Since 1997, when Oregon became the first state to legalize doctor-assisted suicide, more than 340 people have been killed by lethal doses administered by physicians.[25]

The Hippocratic Oath was formulated 2,000 years ago to ensure that patients would know that the doctors who approached their bed would have only one thing in mind: healing them. Government-directed health care that encourages people to get doctors to help them kill themselves violates this biblically sound moral code.

When the Italian dictator Benito Mussolini needed a serious operation, he opted for a Catholic-run hospital, instead of one of the new state-run facilities. When asked why, he said something on the order of, "Because I know that these people will actually try to save my life." In other words, because the staff answered to a higher authority—God Himself—Mussolini had a better chance of getting honest care.

Americans, who polls show strongly (58 percent) favor repeal,[26] need to tell their elected officials in no uncertain terms that they don't want socialized health care. Not if they want to keep this a free republic with the best health care in the world.

TWELVE

Fashioning the Shackles
of Economic Bondage

In his second letter to the Corinthians, the apostle Paul lays out the proper order of financial responsibility:

> And I will not be burdensome to you; for I do not seek yours, but you. For the children ought not to lay up for the parents, but the parents for the children (2 Corinthians 12:14).

Since the New Deal in the 1930s, this generational arrangement has been altered by massive government programs and spending that have mortgaged the economic future of rising generations.

For years, government spending has grown at all levels. By approving ever-larger bond issues and government programs and electing legislators who recklessly spend, voters have been sentencing their grandchildren and great-grandchildren to paying for huge deficits with new taxes.

This profoundly immoral shifting of the burden to future generations has accelerated in recent years as personal and public debt have skyrocketed.

Under President Bush and Congress, the federal deficit grew exponentially.

The abandonment of fiscal control under the GOP-controlled

federal government was a major factor in the American people's decision to return control of Congress to the Democrats in 2006 and the White House in 2008.

But as bad as the federal binge was during the first years of the new millennium, it pales against the spending that has been unleashed by the Obama administration and a newly empowered Democratic Congress. From a Heritage Foundation report:

> President Bush presided over a $2.5 trillion increase in the public debt through 2008. Setting aside 2009 (for which Presidents Bush and Obama share responsibility for an additional $2.6 trillion in public debt), President Obama's budget would add $4.9 trillion in public debt from the beginning of 2010 through 2016.[1]

The administration's promised "change" is coming amid continuing economic turmoil that began with the September 2008 stock market crash and spiraled into the deepest recession in many decades. The political Left is seizing the opening to transfer fiscal power from the private sector to the public sector, particularly to the national government.

President Obama's chief of staff, former Rep. Rahm Emmanuel (D-Ill.), said,

> "You never want a serious crisis to go to waste. ... It's an opportunity to do things that you think you could not do before."[2]

And so they have. Within weeks, building on a multi-billion financial buyout plan designed by the Bush administration, the new administration cobbled together a $788 billion stimulus plan on top of trillions in bailouts for banks, brokerages, insurance firms, and the auto industry—plus an omnibus federal agency spending bill.

Here's a breakdown, courtesy of economic reporter Julie Mason:

> In quick succession, Obama rolled out a $2 trillion financial services bailout, a $788 billion stimulus package, the $13.4 billion preliminary bailout for automakers, a $410 billion spending plan to cover the rest of the current fiscal year, a proposed $275 billion foreclosure rescue plan, and a $3.5 trillion budget that includes a $634 billion fund for health care.[3]

The president and his congressional allies insist that this spending will not send Americans into debt because of "savings" built into the plan. But Heritage Foundation analyst Brian M. Riedl explains that the "savings" may turn out to be illusory:

> During his recent address to a joint session of Congress, President Obama previewed his budget by asserting that the Administration has "already identified $2 trillion in savings over the next decade." This is simply not true. His budget increases spending by $1 trillion over the next decade, which he attempts to offset by reclassifying as "savings" $1.4 trillion in tax increases and $1.5 trillion in reduced spending in Iraq. However, government savings have always referred to spending cuts that save taxpayer dollars, not tax increases that feed the government. Furthermore, the Iraq "savings" are measured against an implausible spending

baseline that assumes a *permanent* $180 billion budget for the global war on terrorism, without any troop withdrawals through 2019. This is the equivalent of a family deciding to "save" $10,000 by first assuming an expensive vacation and then not taking it.[4]

While all this was happening, the Federal Reserve was directed to print more money to begin paying for it. When dollars are printed, while production declines in goods and services, the result is inflation, which is the cruelest tax of all, since it hits people on fixed incomes the hardest. Again and again, Obama has insisted that the government must spend even more to "create jobs." But since the stimulus bill passed in February 2009, more than 2.6 million private jobs were lost, while the government workforce grew by 400,000.[5] The unemployment rate remains stubbornly around 10 percent, with as many as another 7 percent either having given up looking for a job or settling for part-time work.[6]

During the presidential campaign of 2008, both Republican John McCain and Democrat Barack Obama, as well as many congressional candidates, railed against "pork" in the federal budget and promised to end the practice. "Pork" is the slang term for unnecessary expenditures slipped in by legislators looking to buy favor in their own districts or states.

In the very first budget bill—the $410 billion Omnibus Appropriations Act that Congress sent to President Obama in March 2009, pork was everywhere. Combined with the fiscal 2009 budgets of several agencies that were approved in late 2008, the picture was not pretty, as analyzed by Citizens Against Government Waste:

> In fiscal year 2009, Congress stuffed 10,160 projects into the 12 appropriations bills worth $19.6 billion.

The projects represent a 12.5 percent decrease from the 11,610 projects in fiscal year 2008. The $19.6 billion is a 14 percent increase over the fiscal year 2008 total of $17.2 billion, belying claims of reduced spending. Total pork identified by CAGW since 1991 adds up to $290 billion.[7]

Instead of sending it back, Obama signed it, saying he would expect more discipline from Congress in future budget bills, a discipline that did not materialize, as pork flowed into all sorts of subsequent bills.

Several federal agencies, such as Interior and Agriculture, saw their budgets increase by 45 percent in a single fiscal year. The Departments of Labor and Health and Human Services both will had 91 percent increases, and Housing and Urban Development zoomed by 139 percent (owing to the mortgage crisis bailout).[8]

"It's out of hand," said Chris Edwards, director of tax policy for Cato Institute. "I think federal spending is more out of control now than I ever remember it in my 19 years in Washington. It's completely unbelievable what is going on in Washington."[9]

FOLLOWING WEIMAR GERMANY

Although some observers have warned that the federal government's deficit spending is exerting control over the economy in the manner of the New Deal, economics writer James Srodes says that today's pattern more closely fits what happened in Germany after World War I amid the Weimar Republic's economic meltdown. A former Washington bureau chief for *Forbes* and *Financial World* magazines, Srodes observes:

It is commonplace today to believe we should refer to the benign innovations of John Maynard

Keynes during the Great Depression in order to understand what is driving President Obama's team of economic strategists. But a look back to that time leads one to conclude the Depression-era economist who appears most relevant to what is going on bears the improbable name of Hjalmar Horace Greeley Schacht.

From his post as head of the Reichsbank, in a career that ran nearly 20 years, Schacht was in effective control of the shambolic German economy for successive Weimar Republic governments and the pre-World War II regime of Adolf Hitler. During that time he routinely talked one game and ran another.

Srodes takes pains to insist that he is not comparing President Obama to the Nazis in any fashion,[10] only that the president's fiscal policy is strikingly similar to the way Schacht dealt with Germany's monumental economic problems:

Instead of actually trying to take over the formal management of the private sector, the Obama plan is to use the printing presses of the Federal Reserve as a powerful lever to force private enterprise to serve the administration's social agenda. Congress, pacified with pork injections, will have no policy role.[11]

Also looming as a wild card in terms of government expenditures and economic impact are the vast array of measures proposed to curb greenhouse gases in order to reduce allegedly man-made "global warming." After the "cap and trade" bill was sidelined amid the debate over health care, the Environmental Protection Agency took it upon itself in December 2009 to act as the nation's carbon nanny. The EPA declared carbon dioxide and several other "greenhouse gases" to be a "public danger."[12] The agency began formulating ways to regulate businesses via bureaucratic dictate. In response, Sen. Lisa Murkowski (R-Alaska) introduced the Resolution of Disapproval of the Environmental Protection Agency's Endangerment Finding (S.J. Res. 26), but it was defeated in the Senate on June 10, 2010 by a vote of 47-53.[13]

Despite rising public opposition, liberals continue to push the ever more expensive "global warming" agenda, regardless of what it will cost generations to come. As the *Washington Times* editorial page explains:

> [H]igh-cost "green" initiatives pushed by enviro-
> nmental alarmists (the real experts in exploiting
> crises) keep thundering forward like a bowling
> ball aimed at the few standing sectors of our
> economy. The new rules threaten to push up
> the costs of making goods and push down America's
> ability to compete globally.[14]

SUMMARY

The Bible is the ultimate blueprint for fiscal sanity, replete with warnings against reckless lending and getting into debt, and admonitions to respect others' property and to provide for one's own.

As the government grows to claim more and more of each American's income from the sweat of their brow, Caesar grows in power.

In answer to the famous attempt to trap him, Jesus Christ told the Pharisees, "Render therefore to Caesar the things that are Caesar's, and to God the things that are God's" (Matthew 22:21).

As part of our stewardship, we need to hold public officials accountable for how they are spending our tax money and how much of it they are taking. The Lord requires a minimal tithe—that is 10 percent of one's earnings. Being forced to pay more than that to a secular authority, even in a free republic, might arguably be evidence of idolatry.

Every American should pray that the economy recovers so that people can return to work, invest wisely, and provide our children and grandchildren with a bright future. Also, pray that America can continue to shine as a beacon of freedom in a dark world and can generously support missionaries and Christian ministries around the world.

THIRTEEN

How the Resistance
Is Taking Shape

The emergence of the Tea Parties is a clear sign that Americans are aware that they can no longer sit on the sidelines as their country is being transformed into a secular, socialist kleptocracy. The ongoing vitriol directed at the Tea Parties by media and political elites indicates that they are being taken seriously and that they threaten the ruling class.

What appeared to be merely a quixotic, rear-guard reaction against inevitable victory by political "progressives" is becoming a political tidal wave, with much of it still under the opinion makers' radar. It's easy to get discouraged when the radical elites stun us almost daily with new initiatives, so it's good to be reminded of what happened to some other apparently "inevitable" liberal triumphs. Beating tough odds is part of the American spirit. Ordinary citizens have pulled off amazing victories, despite opposition from media, political elites, and powerful corporations. Here are three:

ERA's a slam dunk. Not. During the 1970s, with virtually the entire media, political, and even business establishments backing the Equal Rights Amendment (ERA), an Illinois housewife and writer named Phyllis Schlafly began a crusade to educate Americans about how the ERA posed many threats to women and families. Among other things, she warned, it could mean drafting women into the armed forces, destroying the legal advantages of marriage, ending all restrictions on abortion, abolishing gender distinctions in the law, forcing businesses to open co-ed bathrooms, and to erase family-friendly workplace policies, ending Social Security benefits for housewives, and ushering in the entire homosexual agenda.

More than 30 states had approved the ERA within a year of its introduction in 1972. It needed only 38 for passage. The task of defeating it looked impossible, but Schlafly, through prayer, hard work, a network of supporters and speaking the truth consistently and effectively, turned the tide. She did literally thousands of interviews, spoke coast to coast, and rallied a huge grassroots movement.

From 1972 to 1978, only five more states passed ERA, but five others rescinded it. Feminists held a massive International Women's Year conference in Houston in 1977, but it backfired on them. As Schlafly relates in a 2007 *Los Angeles Times* column,

> When conference delegates voted for taxpayer funding of abortions and the entire gay rights agenda, Americans discovered the ERA's hidden agenda.[1]

Eventually, after a number of extensions, and to the media's astonishment, the measure died—the victim of one woman's remarkable courage and persistence.

What are a few home schoolers against the liberal political machine? In February 1994, the Home School Legal Defense Association (HSLDA) got word that Rep. George Miller (D-Calif.) had inserted into H.R. 6, the appropriations bill for the Elementary and Secondary Education Act (ESEA), a paragraph that would have brought home schoolers under the authority of local educational agencies.

Mike Farris, HSLDA's president, reasoned that this would be the death knell of independent home schooling, and he directed HSLDA to mount a full-court press against it. With liberal Democrats in control of the White House and both houses of Congress, HSDLA faced an uphill battle. But several blast faxes, telephone banks manned by volunteers, and a blitz from Christian and conservative media resulted in more than a million phone calls. Congressional staff reported that the campaign shut down Capitol Hill.

Within days, the House overwhelmingly passed a measure ensuring that the government would not threaten home schooling.[2]

Amnesty for illegals? Not on our watch. In June 2007, the talk show radio waves crackled with the news that a bi-partisan immigration reform bill backed by President Bush and many congressional leaders would essentially give amnesty to 12 million illegal aliens, thus paving the way for another surge of illegal immigration.

For weeks, Capitol Hill was inundated with angry calls, e-mails, and faxes. Politicians who had advocated exotic progressive proposals, such as granting state drivers' licenses to illegal immigrants, backed off their ideas.

On June 28, with 18 senators who voted to advance the bill earlier now switching to vote "no," the bill was defeated.[3] It was a huge victory for grassroots Americans over political elites, and it triggered liberal discussion of bringing back the Fairness Doctrine to silence talk radio.

THE POWER OF CONVICTION

These turnabouts came because Americans believed in their hearts that these proposals violated some of their most deeply held values and acted accordingly. They let public officials know their displeasure in huge numbers. The saying in Washington, state capitals, and even in city councils is: "When they feel the heat, they see the light."

It does not take millions of citizen-activists who are continually engaged to make a difference. It just takes hundreds of thousands who will pray and do one thing a week—or a month—such as calling a legislator. Or e-mailing a company sponsoring an immoral cause or program. Or writing a brief letter to the editor of their local newspaper. Or signing a petition.

But it has to begin with prayer. Nothing good can be accomplished without God's blessing.

People who can afford to be more active can donate to or work on a political campaign or run for office themselves. What a difference it would make if local school boards had majorities of people with traditional values, or even one or two members who would hold the rest accountable.

Individuals can, indeed, make a difference. But the secular Left is counting on sowing discouragement and disorientation among pro-family and conservative Americans.

At the Holocaust Museum in Washington, D.C., a film shows how the German people were, through carefully orchestrated propaganda, co-opted into becoming part of a totalitarian government that committed genocide. Propaganda Minister Joseph Goebbels and his media machine did not have to turn their fellow German citizens into mass murderers; they only had to turn them into *bystanders*. At the same time, they vilified the Jews until the average German felt no obligation to defend his Jewish neighbor, when the Brownshirts began persecuting them and eventually hauling them away to the death camps.

Since the 1960s, the Left has been fighting a culture war designed not to turn Americans into communists, but to turn them into people so fearful of violating the evolving standards of "tolerance" that they have become *bystanders*. More and more people are afraid to engage in honest discussion of public issues, lest they appear to be "haters" or "bigots."

C.S. Lewis once said that the agenda of the Left is to make pornography public and religion private. It's no coincidence that the premiere legal group of the Left, the ACLU, has worked tirelessly to beat down all laws and public policies that uphold public decency.

The explosion in availability of pornography of all kinds has taken many good men off the moral playing field. Ashamed of their weakness in the face of temptation, they decline to get involved in moral issues. One of the devil's best tricks is to persuade people that they are not good enough to act virtuously, because if they did, they would be "hypocrites."

The media love to miscast the church as a place (not a congregation) where people are supposed to become sinless before they even think of walking through the doors. The reality is that the church is a come-as-you-are venture where people cleanse their minds and souls with biblical truth and fellowship. If people waited until they were sin-free, the churches would be utterly empty.

One of the church's main tasks in the face of a relentless secular assault is to shuck the media-fed image of grim-faced hypocrite. That takes genuine humility before God, so that love of God and man can overcome anger, personal weakness, and fear. Love truly does conquer all. We have it on good authority from The Authority.

We also have one more built-in advantage. The devil, being a creature of excess, has a way of overplaying his hand.

Americans were given a gift on April 19, 2009, when "Perez Hilton," the flamboyant homosexual judge at the Miss USA Pageant pilloried Miss California, Carrie Prejean, merely for saying she believes marriage is the union of a man and a woman. He continued to lash out at her for two days, giving Americans a startling look at what the militant gay activists have in mind for the whole nation, should they prevail.

Sometimes, it takes a moment like this to wake people up to

a larger truth, which is that the Left's cultural agenda is not about tolerance at all, but about legitimizing sin and persecuting people who believe in biblical morality.

For her part, Miss Prejean did not react in like manner. Instead, she reiterated her moral stand and forgave Hilton his evil conduct toward her.

> I knew at that moment after I answered the question, I knew I was not going to win because of my answer, because I had spoken from my heart, from my beliefs and for my God," she told Matt Lauer on NBC's *Today Show*. "....I wouldn't have answered it differently. The way I answered may have been offensive. With that question specifically, it's not about being politically correct. For me it was being biblically correct.[4]

On the Fox News Channel's *Hannity* program, Prejean said of Hilton, "You know, I forgive him. I know that he's angry, for whatever reason. I know there must be a bigger issue going on in his life."[5]

Instead of going down in history as one more forgotten Miss USA, Carrie will instead be remembered as someone who did not back down from her faith, speaking the truth in love. She continued to do so in the face of a vicious, concerted campaign to discredit her over some earlier bad decisions in her life. Stands like that have both eternal and earthly consequences.

WHAT WE ARE UP AGAINST

The pro-family movement rose in the 1970s not because people disliked homosexuals or hated abortionists, but because the Left had gone beyond asking for tolerance of sin on an individual level and had begun harnessing government power to legitimize sin. The

Left's progress was stalled politically for a time, but the cultural war waged by Hollywood and the educational establishment continued unabated. Now that the Left has regained the levers of national political power, they are using it forcefully.

From the moment they took office, the Congress and the Administration began initiating radical proposals in rapid-fire succession. Anyone not embracing them was accused of being unpatriotic. Not a day passed without news of yet another radical attempt to reorder America's economy or culture. The idea was to create so many battlefronts at once that people could not get organized to mount a resistance. The risk was that the sheer volume of "change" would wake up people to see that despite all the "moderate" rhetoric, the actual legislation, appointments, and policies veered sharply left.

Without alternative media, such as talk radio, Christian Web sites, Internet news sites and blogs, Americans would be uninformed about key developments. The "mainstream" media have become embarrassingly partisan and do not seem to care that anyone knows.

Journalists laugh if you suggest the possibility of a left-wing media conspiracy, but in July 2010, the conservative Daily Caller Website unearthed one. From 2007 to June 2010, 400 liberal journalists and policy experts exchanged ideas on how to ensure liberal political victories. They were particularly adamant about advancing and defending Barack Obama. The e-mail list called Journolist contained a number of revealing outbursts by working journalists. Here's one as reported by *The Wall Street Journal's* John Fund:

> Spencer Ackerman, then of the *Washington Independent*, now at *Wired* [magazine], urged fellow journalists to kill the story of Mr. Obama's ties to the controversial Reverend Jeremiah Wright by going after some of his critics.
>
> "Fred Barnes, Karl Rove, who cares—and call

them racists," he urged. "What is necessary is to raise the cost on the right of going after the left. In other words, find a right-winger's [sic] and smash it through a plate-glass window. Take a snapshot of the bleeding mess and send it out in a Christmas card to let the right know that it needs to live in a state of constant fear. Obviously, I mean this rhetorically."[6]

This is what passes for media tolerance of other points of view. But the media are paying a price for their haughty indifference to their own bias. TV broadcast networks are losing market share, and major newspapers like *The New York Times* are in deep financial trouble and losing readers. Although spokespeople blame it on the rise of the Internet, there is a case to be made that readers and viewers, tired of liberal bias, are going elsewhere because they finally have a choice.

The window is closing on a day when CBS, NBC, and ABC can lull Americans into complacency by repeating leftwing talking points and airing unflattering portrayals of public figures they don't like.

CBS anchor Dan Rather found out the hard way that the new media have teeth. After he aired a segment accusing President Bush of having cheated on his Air National Guard training, a blogger ran an item revealing that the so-called authoritative document at the center of the charge had, in fact, been printed on Microsoft Word, a technology that had not existed when Mr. Bush was in his training in the 1970s. Busted![7]

CBS was forced to air a clarification, and Dan Rather lost his job as his ratings plunged.

The rise of the new media means that journalistic or political misconduct will be far harder to cover up. Another reason to be of good cheer in the face of the radical left Blitzkrieg is that America, for all its faults, has a reservoir of traditional values and is the most religious of all industrialized nations. America has a Christian remnant that has yet to be reckoned with.

Americans soundly rejected liberalism in the 1980s, so much so that liberals had to abandon the word "liberal." It has become shorthand for socialism, American weakness, sexual perversion, and hatred of Christianity. That's why liberals now call themselves "progressives."

When you have to keep changing the terms, you are losing the debate. The key to winning future battles will be to identify and label radically liberal proposals for what they are and to rally Americans to oppose them.

We are witnessing what is becoming a massive case of buyer's remorse, as people realize how wide the gap is between their values and those of the current political leadership.

After months of enacting radical legislation in the face of majority American opposition, Congress has sunk to new lows in terms of public esteem. Gallup's 2010 Confidence in Institutions poll rated Congress last out of 16 institutions. The military continued to be at the top of the list, with 76 percent reporting a "high level of confidence" in the armed forces, followed by small businesses (66 percent), the police (59 percent), and "the church as organized religion" (48 percent). As for Congress, only 11 percent said they had a "great deal" or "quite a lot" of confidence in the law makers. The presidency under Barack Obama also showed a serious slippage in popularity, dropping from 51 percent in June 2009 to 36 percent in June 2010.[8]

The public's dissatisfaction with the ruling elites is spurring an enormous amount of political activity.

Conservatives won governorships in off-year elections in 2009 in Virginia and New Jersey. On January 19, 2010, Republican upstart candidate Scott Brown won the Massachusetts U.S. Senate seat formerly held by Ted Kennedy for four decades. The overriding issue was government spending, and the health care takeover in particular. This addition of a 41st Republican Senate vote eliminated the Democrats' ability to easily end GOP filibusters

An estimated one million Americans rallied to hold Tea Parties on April 15, 2009, in more than 880 cities.[9] The Tea Party crowd at a rally on Sept. 12, 2009, on the Mall in Washington, D.C., was widely estimated between several hundred thousand and 1.5 million,[10] with another major event planned for September 12, 2010, at the Washington Monument. The massive 2009 event, which I attended with my wife, was concurrent with the national Black Family Reunion, whose tents dominated the middle of the mall. If any media people were hoping to witness and record racial incidents, they were sorely disappointed. Hundreds of thousands of Americans for two entirely different events and of largely different racial groups gathered peaceably in the shadow of the Capitol.

Fox News personality Glenn Beck broadcast his program from a rally the same day at the Alamo in San Antonio. He noted on air that although the local media had estimated the crowd at around 4,000, the Alamo staff's estimate was 20,000.

Later, as the health care bill was being debated, another 20,000 gathered at the U.S. Capitol on Nov. 4, a weekday, to protest ObamaCare. The rally, which I also attended, was peaceful and spirited.

Despite the plethora of peaceful Tea Party events nationwide, the media, politicians and leftist groups continued to try to paint many Americans as racist and extremist.

In April 2010, Mr. Obama blasted Arizona for passing a statute requiring state and local police to help enforce federal immigration law. On April 27, he fanned Hispanic fears by saying: "Suddenly, if you don't have your papers and you took your kid out to get ice cream, you're going to be harassed."[11] The law bars racial profiling and allows officers to ask for proof of legal immigration during legal stops and arrests. Americans overwhelmingly support the Arizona law, and nine states have filed a brief supporting Arizona. States such as Rhode Island have been checking immigration status during traffic stops for years.

Eric Holder and Homeland Security Secretary Janet Napolitano also excoriated the 10-page law, admitting later that they hadn't read it.[12] Mr. Holder sued Arizona on July 6, claiming the law violates the Constitution's supremacy clause.[13] Remember, this is a state law aimed at enforcing federal law, not flouting it. And speaking of flouting the law, Justice spokeswoman Tracy Schmaler told *The Washington Times* that "sanctuary cities" that won't cooperate with federal authorities would face no action.[14]

On July 13, 2010, the NAACP unveiled a resolution, with scant proof, charging the Tea Parties with harboring "racist elements."[15] But the most openly racist incidents were occurring courtesy of the Obama Administration, whose Justice Department dismissed serious charges against New Black Panther Party members who had been caught on videotape in military garb and wielding what prosecutors called a "deadly weapon" at a Philadelphia polling place on Nov. 4, 2008.

One defendant, King Samir Shabbazz, who wore military garb and brandished a baton, later told a black audience, "You want freedom? You're gonna have to kill some crackers. You're gonna have to kill some of their babies."[16] In case anyone missed his point, he also said, "I hate white people—all of them."[17] Given that Eric Holder was a prime proponent of passing the federal hate crimes bill, one would think that Mr. Shabbazz might stay on his radar screen.

It gets worse. Justice Department officials were ordered not to prosecute any cases involving minority defendants, according to J. Christian Adams, a former Justice Department attorney who resigned in protest.[18] Testifying on July 6, 2010, before the U.S. Civil Rights Commission, Mr. Adams said that Deputy Assistant Attorney General Julie Fernandes had announced that "the Voting Section will not bring any other cases against blacks and other minorities."[19]

The left has always prospered by pitting groups against each other. But Americans aren't buying it this time. The NAACP's charge against the Tea Parties has fallen flat. If anything, it has made that once-estimable group more irrelevant. And Mr. Adams' testimony has "outed" the Justice Department's overt racism, putting it on notice.

TAKE HEART, TAKE ACTION

At the opening of this chapter, we related several instances in which Americans rallied to defeat proposals that threatened their nation's well-being.

Today, Americans can rally the same way to defeat radical "reforms" that all amount to more government control at the expense of families, churches, and free enterprise.

To do so, we need to recover a robust sense of who we are and why America became the freest, wealthiest, and most generous nation in history. It began with a firm belief in Judeo-Christian spiritual truths. In that Calvin Coolidge speech referenced in the beginning of this book, the 30th president showed why we neglect our heritage at our own peril:

> In its main feature the Declaration of Independence is a great spiritual document. It is a declaration not of material but of spiritual conceptions. Equality, liberty, popular sovereignty, the rights of man—these are ... ideals. They have their source and their roots in the religious convictions. They belong to the unseen world. Unless the faith of the American in these religious convictions is to en-

dure, the principles of our Declaration will perish. We can not continue to enjoy the result if we neglect and abandon the cause.[20]

An amusing TV ad a few years ago showed several men up to their waists in a warehouse full of almonds, with each of them, ostensibly an almond grove owner, holding a can of their product. The spokesman half-jokingly said, "All we're asking is one can a week."

In the fight to save America's soul, if Christians and like-minded citizens did one thing a month, it could turn this nation around. And it must continue regardless of the results of our two-year and four-year election cycles, because it is about far more than politics. It is about what kind of country we are leaving to our children and grandchildren.

It's time to get on our knees and ask God's forgiveness and blessing. Then, we need to roll up our sleeves and get the job done.

ENDNOTES

Introduction

1   Public Law 111-148, at: http://www.gpo.gov/fdsys/pkg/PLAW-111publ148/
    content-detail.html.

2   Public Law 18 U.S.C. § 249, at: http://www.justice.gov/crt/crim/249fin.php.

3   "U.S. Department of Education Marks Historic Day in Higher Education," U.S.
    Department of Education press release, July 1, 2010, at http://www.ed.gov/news/
    press-releases/us-department-education-marks-historic-day-higher-education.

4   Daniel de Vise, "House approves huge changes to student loan program," *The
    Washington Post*, March 22, 2010, at: http://www.washingtonpost.com/wp-dyn/
    content/article/2010/03/21/AR2010032103548.html.

5   David M. Dickson, "CBO report: Debt will rise to 90% of GDP," *The Washington
    Times*, March 26, 2010, at: http://www.washingtontimes.com/news/2010/mar/26/
    cbos-2020-vision-debt-will-rise-to-90-of-gdp/.

6   Brian Brown, "President Obama and Elena Kagan Sabotage DOMA Defense," The
    Daily Caller, July 13, 2010, at: http://dailycaller.com/2010/07/13/president-obama-
    and-elena-kagan-sabotage-doma-defense/.

7   Michael O'Brien, "Obama orders extension of benefits to gay and lesbian federal
    employees," The Hill, June 2, 2010, at: http://thehill.com/blogs/blog-briefing-
    room/news/101149-obama-signs-memo-extending-benefits-to-gay-and-lesbian-
    federal-employees.

8   Sheryl Gay Stolberg, "Obama Vows Progress on Gay Rights Agenda," *The New York
    Times*, June 22, 2010, at: http://thecaucus.blogs.nytimes.com/2010/06/22/obama-
    vows-progress-on-gay-rights-agenda/.

9   Chris Harris, "Barack Obama Answers Your Questions About Gay Marriage,
    Paying for College, More," MTV.com, Nov. 1, 2008, at http://www.mtv.com/news/
    articles/1598407/20081101/story.jhtml.

10 Maura Dolan and Carol Williams, "Judge strikes down Prop 8, allows gay marriage
    in California," *Los Angeles Times*, Aug. 4, 2010, at: http://www.latimes.com/news/
    local/la-mew-prop-8-10042010,0,7711145.story?track=rss.

11 Mary Beth Sheridan and Colum Lynch, "Obama administration discloses size of U.S.
    nuclear arsenal, *The Washington Post*, May 4, 2010, at: http://www.washingtonpost.
    com/wp-dyn/content/article/2010/05/03/AR2010050302089.html.

12 Dan Buecke, "House Passes Carbon Cap-and-Trade Bill," *Bloomberg Businessweek*,
    June 25, 2009, at: http://www.businessweek.com/blogs/money_politics/
    archives/2009/06/house_passes_ca.html.

13   Sindya N. Bhanoo, "E.P.A. Announces a New Rule on Polluters," *The New York Times*, May 13, 2010, at: http://www.nytimes.com/2010/05/14/science/earth/14permit.html.

14   Jill Jackson, "House Passes DISCLOSE ACT," CBSNEWS.com, June 24, 2010, at: http://www.cbsnews.com/8301-503544_162-20008783-503544.html.

15   Greg Hitt and Brody Mullins, "Contribution-Disclosure Measure Fails Senate Test Vote," *The Wall Street Journal* online, July 27, 2010, at: http://online.wsj.com/article/SB10001424052748703977004575393541649256712.html?mod=googlenews_wsj.

16   Calvin Coolidge, address at the 150th Anniversary of the Declaration of Independence, Philadelphia, July 5, 1926, quoted in William J. Federer, *Three Secular Reasons Why America Should Be Under God* (St. Louis: Amerisearch, Inc., 2008), p. 34.

17   President John Adams, Letter to the Third Division of the Militia of Massachusetts, Oct. 11, 1798, quoted in Federer, p. 36.

18   Thomas Jefferson, Query XVIII, Notes on the State of Virginia, 1781, quoted in Federer, p. 15, and at: http://www.monticello.org/reports/quotes/memorial.html.

19   Chelsea Schilling, "Is this man Obama's worst nightmare?" WorldNetDaily.com, July 21, 2010, at: http://www.wnd.com/?pageId=181961.

Chapter One

1   "Thomas Jefferson on Politics & Government," at: http://etext.virginia.edu/jefferson/quotations/jeff0650.htm.

2   "Hippocratic Oath," Greek Medicine, History of Medicine Division, National Library of Medicine, National Institutes of Health, at: http://www.nlm.nih.gov/hmd/greek/greek_oath.html. A pessary is a device inserted into a woman's vagina for medical purposes, but which could also cause abortions.

3   The Hippocratic Oath, Modern Version, NOVA, Public Broadcasting Service, at: http://www.pbs.org/wgbh/nova/doctors/oath_modern.html.

4   Ibid.

5   D. James Kennedy, Jerry Newcombe, *Lord of All: Developing a Christian World-and-Life View* (Wheaton, Ill: Crossway Books, 2005), p. 77.

6   Jessica Wadkins, Trudy Chun, Catherina Hurlburt, "History of Abortion," Concerned Women for America, December 1999, at: http://www.cwfa.org/articledisplay.asp?id=1416&department=CWA&categoryid=life.

7   Dr. and Mrs. J.C. Wilke, *Why Can't We Love Them Both?*, Chapter 7, "Legal Pre-Roe," (Heritage House, 1976). Also available at: http://www.abortionfacts.com/online_books/love_them_both/why_cant_we_love_them_both_7.asp.

8   Judith A. Reisman and Edward W. Eichel, *Kinsey, Sex and Fraud: the Indoctrination of a People* (Lafayette, Louisiana: Huntington House, 1990).

9   Judith A. Reisman, *Kinsey: Crimes & Consequences* (Crestwood, Kentucky: Institute for Media Education, 1998, 2000), p. 187.

10   Samuel Kling, *Sexual Behavior & The Law* (New York: Random House, 1965), p. 9, cited in Riesman, *Kinsey: Crimes & Consequences*, p. 246.

11   Robert Marshall, Charles Donovan, *Blessed Are the Barren: The Social Policy of Planned Parenthood* (San Francisco: Ignatius Press, 1991), p. 247.

12   Wilke, op. cit.

13   Kathryn Jean Lopez, "The Greening of Planned Parenthood," National Review Online, June 23, 2008, at: http://article.nationalreview.com/?q=ZWU1YmMzNWVh MTFhYTQxNjliZGIxMTcxYWU2NTMynNTQ=.

Chapter Two

1   "Rightwing Extremism: Current Economic and Political Climate Fueling Resurgence in Radicalization and Recruitment," U.S. Department of Homeland Security, April 7, 2009, p.2, at: http://www.fas.org/irp/eprint/rightwing.pdf.

2   Samantha Singson, "Obama Admin Calls for Universal Access to Abortion at United Nations Meeting," Lifenews.com, July 2, 2009, at: http://www.lifenews.com/ int1255.html.

3   Steven Ertelt, "President Barack Obama's Pro-Abortion Record: A Pro-Life Compilation," Lifenews.com, March 7, 2010 and continually updated, at: http://www. lifenews.com/obamaabortionrecord.html.

4   Michael Gerson, "Why Obama Is Losing a Faith," *The Washington Post*, April 1, 2009, p. A-21.

5   Bernadine Healy, M.D., "Why Embryonic Stem Cells Are Obsolete," *U.S. News & World Report*, March 4, 2009, at: http://health.usnews.com/blogs/heart-to-heart/2009/03/04/why-embryonic-stem-cells-are-obsolete_print.htm.

6   Ronald Reagan, "Abortion and the Conscience of a Nation," *Human Life Review*, Spring 1983.

7   Ibid.

Chapter Three

1   Richard Grenier, *Capturing the Culture: Film, Art and Politics* (Washington, D.C.: Ethics and Public Policy Center, 1991), p. xiv.

2   Robert Knight, *The Age of Consent: The Rise of Relativism and the Corruption of Popular Culture* (Dallas: Spence Publishing, 1998, 2000), p. 125, 176.

3   Grenier, p. xiv.

4   Ibid., p. xivii.

5   Not "idealistic." The term is used by Pitirim Sorokin to describe the move away from religion-based values to hedonism.

6   Pitirim Sorokin, *The Crisis of Our Age: The Social and Cultural Outlook* (New York: E.P. Dutton, Inc., 1941), p. 242.

7   Joseph Daniel Unwin, *Sexual Regulations and Cultural Behaviour* (Trona, Calif.: Frank Darrow, 1969), p. 32.

8   Ibid., p. 34.

9   Pitirim Sorokin, *The American Sexual Revolution* (Boston: Porter Sargent Publisher, 1956), p. 28.

10   Ibid., p. 24.

11   D. James Kennedy, Jerry Newcombe, *Lord of All: Developing a Christian World-and-*

Life View (Wheaton, Illinois: Crossway Books, 2005), p. 286.

Chapter Four

1   Ronald Bayer, *Homosexuality and American Psychiatry: The Politics of Diagnosis* (New York: Basic Books, 1981), quoted in Charles Socarides, *A Freedom Too Far* (Phoenix: Adam Margrave Books, 1995), pp. 165, 166.

2   "Dr. Jeffrey Satinover Testifies Before Massachusetts Senate Committee Studying Gay Marriage," April 28, 2003, at http://www.narth.com/docs/senatecommittee.html.

3   Robert H. Knight, *The Age of Consent: The Rise of Relativism and the Corruption of Popular Culture* (Dallas: Spence Publishing, 1998, 2000), p. 63.

4   *Baehr v. Lewin*, 852 P.2d 44 (Haw. 1993).

5   *Romer v. Evans* (1994) at: http://caselaw.lp.findlaw.com/scripts/getcase.pl?court=US &vol=000&invol=u10179.

6   Jeffrey Satinover, M.D., "The Trojan Couch: How the Mental Health Associations Misrepresent Science," undated paper, National Association for the Research and Therapy of Homosexuality at: http://www.narth.com/docs/TheTrojanCouch Satinover.pdf.

7   *Goodridge v. Department of Public Health*, Massachusetts Supreme Judicial Court, Nov. 18, 2003, at: http://fl1.findlaw.com/news.findlaw.com/wp/docs/conlaw/ goodridge111803opn.pdf.

8   *Kerrigan v. Commissioner of the Public Health* at: http://www.jud.state.ct.us/external/ supapp/Cases/AROcr/CR289/289CR152.pdf.

9   *Varnum v. Brien*, Iowa Supreme Court, April 3, 2009, p.11, at: http://www.politico. com/static/PPM104_090403_iowacourt.html.

10   Robert Lerner, Ph.D., Althea Nagai, Ph.D., *No Basis: What the studies don't tell us about same-sex parenting* (Washington, D.C.: Marriage Law Project, 2001).

11   Michelangelo Signorile, "Bridal Wave," *OUT* magazine, December/January 1994, p. 161.

12   Chai Feldblum, "Moral Conflict and Liberty: Gay Rights and Religion," paper delivered at Becket Fund for Religious Liberty symposium, 2005, p. 17, at: http:// www.becketfund.org/files/4bce5.pdf. Originally published in the *Brooklyn Law Review* (72) 61 (2006).

13   Ibid., p. 2.

Chapter Five

1   Karl Marx, *The Communist Manifesto* (Chicago: Henry Regnery Company, 1989, originally published in 1848), pp. 48, 49.

2   G. K. Chesterton, *The Superstition of Divorce*, in *Collected Works* Vol. IV, *Family, Society, Politics* (San Francisco: Ignatius Press, 1987), pp. 259, 260. Quoted in Allan Carlson, "Love Is Not Enough: Toward a Recovery of Family Economics," Witherspoon Lecture, June 28, 2002, Family Research Council, at: http://www.frc. org/get.cfm?i=WT02J1#edn7.

3   Frederich Engels, *Origins of the Family, Private Property and the State*, "The Monogamous Family" in Chapter Two, The Family, Marx/Engels Selected

Works, Vol. 3, Marx/Engels Internet Archive, at: http://www.marxists.org/archive/marx/works/1884/origin-family/ch02d.htm.

4   Ibid.

5   Ibid.

6   Allan Carlson, "The Economics of Abortion," Feb. 11, 2006, speech, The Howard Center at: http://www.profam.org/docs/acc/thc.acc.060211.econ.abort.htm?search=family%20tax%20&opt=EXACT.

7   Charles Murray, *Losing Ground: American Social Policy 1950-1980* (New York: Basic Books, 1984), p. 126.

8   Ibid.

9   Ibid., p. 127.

10   Ibid.

11   Ibid., p. 126.

12   National Institutes of Health, "Percentage of live births to unmarried mothers: United States, each state and territory, final 2006 and preliminary 2007" at http://www.cdc.gov/nchs/data/nvsr/nvsr57/nvsr57_12.pdf.

13   Ibid.

14   Robert Rector, "Stimulus Bill Abolishes Welfare Reform and Adds New Welfare Spending," Heritage Foundation, Washington, D.C., Feb. 11, 2009, at http://www.heritage.org/research/welfare/wm2287.cfm.

15   Ibid.

Chapter Six

1   Robert Rector, "Fourteen Myths About Families and Child Care," *Harvard Journal on Legislation* 26 (1989): 517-47.

2   "April 13 Is Tax Freedom Day," Tax Foundation Special Report, April 2009, at http://www.taxfoundation.org/files/sr165.pdf.

3   Martin Feldstein, "A Deduction From Charity," *The Washington Post*, March 25, 2009, p. A-15.

4   Ibid.

Chapter Seven

1   "Kagan's partial-birth extremism," editorial, *The Washington Times*, June 30, 2010, at: http://www.washingtontimes.com/news/2010/jun/30/kagans-partial-birth-extremism/.

2   Andrew C. McCarthy, "Elena Kagan's 'Don't Ask, Don't Tell' Sharia Policy, *National Review* online, July 8, 2010, at: http://article.nationalreview.com/437760/elena-kagans-dont-ask-dont-tell-sharia-policy/andrew-c-mccarthy?page=1.

3   Frank Gaffney, Jr. "Courting Shariah," Center for Security Policy, June 21, 2010, and at Townhall.com at: http://townhall.com/columnists/FrankGaffney/2010/06/21/courting_shariah.

4   Ibid.

5   *All the President's Men & Women: The People and Politics of the Obama Administration,* Coral Ridge Ministries, 2009, p. 2.

6   Neil A. Lewis, "Moderate Said to Be Pick for Court," *The New York Times*, at: http://www.nytimes.com/2009/03/17/us/politics/17nominate.html.

7   John Berry, Memorandum from Office of Personnel Management, "Implementation of the President's Memorandum Regarding Extension of Benefits to Same-Sex Domestic Partners of Federal Employees," June 2, 2010, at: http://www.chcoc.gov/transmittals/TransmittalDetails.aspx?TransmittalID=2982.

8   Public Law 104-199, 104th Congress, The Defense of Marriage Act, at: http://frwebgate.access.gpo.gov/cgi-bin/getdoc.cgi?dbname=104_cong_public_laws&docid=f:publ199.104.pdf.

9   "OPM Director John Berry Lauds Signing of Presidential Memorandum on the Extension of Benefits to Same-Sex Domestic Partners of Federal Employees, press release, U.S. Office of Personnel Management, June 2, 2010, at: http://boston.bizjournals.com/prnewswire/press_releases/District_of_Columbia/2010/06/02/DC14869.

10 Major Garrett, "Energy Secretary Offers Dire Global Warming Prediction," FoxNews.com, April 19, 2009, at: http://www.foxnews.com/politics/first100days/2009/04/19/energy-secretary-offers-dire-global-warming-prediction/.

11 Jonathan Weisman, "Geithner's Tax History Muddles Confirmation," *The Wall Street Journal*, January 9, 2009, at: http://online.wsj.com/article/SB123187503629378119.html.

12 Pierre Thomas and Jason Ryan, "Stinging Remarks on Race from Attorney General," ABC News, Feb. 18, 2009, at: http://abcnews.go.com/TheLaw/Story?id=6905255&page=1.

13 Jerry Markon and Michael D. Shear, "Justice Department sues Arizona over immigration law," *The Washington Post*, July 6, 2010, at: http://www.washingtonpost.com/wp-dyn/content/article/2010/07/06/AR2010070601928.html.

14 J. Christian Adams, "Inside the Black Panther Case," *The Washington Times*, June 25, 2010, at: http://www.washingtontimes.com/news/2010/jun/25/inside-the-black-panther-case-anger-ignorance-and-/.

15 "Filibuster a radical," editorial, *The Washington Times*, April 22, 2009, p. A-20, at: http://washingtontimes.com/news/2009/apr/22/filibuster-a-radical/.

16 Ibid.

17 "Berkeley's Goodwin Liu Nominated to Ninth Circuit," BerkeleyLaw, Feb. 24, 2010, at: http://www.law.berkeley.edu/7806.htm.

18 Bob Egelko, "Majority of D.A.s in state oppose Obama nominee," *San Francisco Chronicle*, March 30, 2010, at: http://www.sfgate.com/cgi-bin/article.cgi?f=/c/a/2010/03/29/BA8U1CN27K.DTL#ixzz0v0n96Kly.

19 "Berkeley's Judge: A liberal nominee of illiberal temperament," editorial, *The Wall Street Journal*, April 17, 2010, at: http://online.wsj.com/article_email/SB10001424052702303491304575188013562799740-lMyQjAxMTAwMDEwNzExNDcyWj.html.

20 Charlie Savage, "Liu Nomination Advances," The Caucus, *The New York Times*, May 12, 2010, at: http://thecaucus.blogs.nytimes.com/2010/05/13/liu-nomination-advances/.

Chapter Eight

1   David Hackworth, "The Case for a Military Gay Ban: My Combat Experience Tells
    Me It's the Only Sensible Policy," *The Washington Post*, June 28, 1992, p. C-5.
2   Pub. L. No. 103-160, § 546, 107 Stat. 1670 (1993) (codified at 10 U.S.C. A. § 654
    (West Supp. 1995)).
3   The White House Web site at: http://www.whitehouse.gov/issues/civil_rights/.
4   Brian Witte, Associated Press, "Admirals, Generals: Repeal 'Don't Ask, Don't Tell.'"
    Nov. 17, 2008, at: http://abcnews.go.com/US/wireStory?id=6274139.
5   Dana Milbank, "Sorry We Asked, Sorry You Told," *The Washington Post,* July 24,
    2008, P. A-3.
6   Military Readiness Enhancement Act (HR 1283) at: http://www.govtrack.us/
    congress/bill.xpd?bill=h111-1283.
7   Quoted in Robert Knight, "The Lady Was Unruffled," *Citizen* magazine, October
    2008, p. 25.
8   Flag and General Officers for the Military website at: http://flagandgeneralofficersfor
    themilitary.com/.
9   Ibid.
10 Jeff Quinton, "ACLU Asks Naval Academy to End Noon Prayers," *Baltimore Sun,*
    June 25, 2008, at: http://insidecharmcity.com/2008/06/25/aclu-asks-naval-academy-
    to-end-noon-prayers/. Also see "U.S. Navy Asked by ADL to End Lunchtime
    Prayers," *Religious Diversity News,* June 24, 2005, at http://pluralism.org/news/article.
    php?id=9934.
11 Brian Mitchell, "Sex and Gender in the Military," broadcast version of an article
    in *American Orthodoxy,* Winter 1993, Ethics and Public Policy Center,
    Washington, D.C.
12 Elaine Donnelly, "Constructing the Co-Ed Military," *Duke Journal of Gender Law &
    Policy*, Vol. 14, May 2007, p. 150, footnote # 851.
13 Testimony of Col. Patrick Toffler, director of West Point's Office of Institutional
    Research, in *United States of America vs. Virginia Military Institute et al,* U.S. District
    Court for the Western District of Virginia, Roanoke Division, April 8, 1991, p. 539,
    as cited in Robert Knight, "Women in Combat: Why Rush to Judgment?"
    Backgrounder, The Heritage Foundation, No. 836, June 14, 1991, pp. 6, 7.
14 Edward N. Luttwak, Center for Strategic and International Studies, Washington,
    D.C., in telephone interview with the author on June 10, 1991, as well as Israeli
    military sources cited in Knight, "Women in Combat," p. 10.
15 Kate O'Beirne, Presidential Commission Report, referencing SERE trainers'
    testimony before the commission on June 8, 1992, and cited in Elaine Donnelly,
    "Constructing the Co-Ed Military," p. 930.
16 Ibid., pp. 815-952.
17 *Rostker v. Goldberg* 453 U.S. 57 (1981) at: http://www1.american.edu/dgolash/
    rostker.htm.
18 Ibid., at 35.
19 David Horowitz, *The Feminist Assault on the Military* (Center for the Study of Popular
    Culture, 1992), p. 20.

20   Ibid.

Chapter Nine

1   Mark Steyn, "Who will lead the 'post-American era'?", April 24, 2009, in the *Orange County Register* at: http://www.ocregister.com/articles/world-american-obama-2375027-exceptionalism-post.

2   George Washington, Farewell Address, Sept. 19, 1796, in Paul M. Angle, *By These Words* (New York: Rand McNally, 1954), p. 147.

3   Ibid., pp. 148-149.

4   United Nations Treaty Collection at: http://treaties.un.org/Pages/Treaties. aspx?id=4&subid=A&lang=en.

5   http://www2.ohchr.org/english/law/crc.htm.

6   Convention on the Rights of the Child, UNICEF, United Nations, at: http://www.unicef.org/crc/.

7   Ibid.

8   "UN Rights of the Child," article, Concerned Women for America, Aug. 7, 1997, at: http://www.cwfa.org/articles/1839/CWA/nation/index.htm.

9   "Violence in the Home and Family," United Nations, undated, p. 51, at: http://www.violencestudy.org/IMG/pdf/3._World_Report_on_Violence_against_Children.pdf.

10   John Goddard, "Spanking Decision May Hit Home," *Toronto Star*, Jan. 24, 2004, at: http://www.nospank.net/n-l33r.htm.

11   Germany, in Global Initiative to End All Corporal Punishment of Children, at: http://www.endcorporalpunishment.org/pages/progress/prohib_states.html.

12   "The Truth About Spanking/Hitting," End Corporal Punishment in the Home Now, Jan. 24, 2007, at http://stophitting.blogspot.com/2007_01_01_archive.html.

13   "Spanking-Ban Plan Threatens Parental Rights," WorldNetDaily.com, Feb. 24, 2007, at: http://www.worldnetdaily.com/news/article.asp?ARTICLE_ID=54417.

14   Laura MacLeod, Catherina Hurlburt, "Exposing CEDAW," Concerned Women for America, Sept. 1, 2000, at: http://www.cwfa.org/articles/1971/CWA/nation/index.htm#ref_1-20#ref_1-20.

15   Ibid.

16   Ibid.

17   Doug Bandow, "The Ultimate in Paper Guarantees," *American Spectator*, April 17, 2009, at: http://spectator.org/archives/2009/04/17/the-ultimate-in-paper-guarante/.

18   "Industrialized Nations to Cut Greenhouse Gases by 5.2%," press release, United Nations, Dec. 11, 1997, at: http://unfccc.int/cop3/fccc/info/indust.htm.

19   "Bush: Kyoto treaty would have hurt economy," AP, at MSNBC.com at : http://www.msnbc.msn.com/id/8422343/.

20   Rick Santorum, "Obama vs. the United States," Ethics and Public Policy Center, April 9, 2009, at: http://www.eppc.org/publications/pubID.3784/pub_detail.asp.

21   Justice Anthony Kennedy, Majority opinion, *Lawrence v. Texas* (June 26, 2003), p. 12 at: http://www.law.cornell.edu/supct/pdf/02-102P.ZO.

22   Justice Anthony Kennedy, Majority opinion, *Roper v. Simmons*, (March 1, 2005), p. 2, at http://www.law.cornell.edu/supct/pdf/03-633P.ZO.

23   Juvenile Death Penalty Amicus Briefs, American Bar Association at: http://www.
      abanet.org/crimjust/juvjus/simmons/simmonsamicus.html.
24   Justice Antonin G. Scalia, dissenting, in *Roper v. Simmons*, p. 14, at: http://www.law.
      cornell.edu/supct/pdf/03-633P.ZD1.
25   Adam Liptak, "Ginsburg Shares Views on Influence of Foreign Law on Her
      Court and Vice Versa," *The New York Times*, April 11, 2009, at: http://www.nytimes.
      com/2009/04/12/us/12ginsburg.html.
26   "O'Connor: U.S. Must Rely on Foreign Law," WorldNetDaily.com, Oct. 31, 2003, at:
      http://www.worldnetdaily.com/news/article.asp?ARTICLE_ID=35367.
27   Ibid., p. 2.

Chapter Ten
1   Herbert Marcuse, "Repressive Tolerance," in: Robert Paul Wolff, Barrington
      Moore, jr., and Herbert Marcuse, *A Critique of Pure Tolerance* (Boston: Beacon
      Press, 1969), pp. 95-137 at: http://www.marcuse.org/herbert/pubs/60spubs/65repressi
      vetolerance.htm.
2   Ibid.
3   Don Feder, "Simian Students Throw Feces at Conservative Speakers," April 7, 2009,
      at Don Feder's Cold Steel Caucus Web site at: http://www.donfeder.com/
      articles/0904%20MeSpeak.pdf.
4   "Loud homosexual activists disrupt and halt Don Feder speech at UMass
      Amherst, despite police presence," Massresistance, March 13, 2009, at: http://www.
      massresistance.org/docs/gen/09a/feder_0311/index.html.
5   Don Feder at: http://www.donfeder.com/.
6   Feder, "Simian Students," op. cit.
7   Andrew Dunn, "Campus protests cause big free speech stir," *The Daily Tar Heel*,
      April 26, 2009, at http://www.dailytarheel.com/news/university/campus-protests-
      cause-big-free-speech-stir-1.1734317.
8   Ibid.
9   Adam Kissel, "Victory for Individual Rights at Pomona College: No-Trespassing
      Order Reversed for Two Students Who Asked 'Disruptive' Questions," *The Torch*,
      March 11, 2009, Foundation for Individual Rights in Education, at: http://www.
      thefire.org/index.php/article/10312.html.
10   "Lesbian activists at Smith College riot, shut down Ryan Sorba speech on 'The Born
      Gay Hoax' as police watch," Massresistance, April 29, 2008, at:http://www.
      massresistance.org/docs/gen/08a/born_gay_hoax/smith_0329/index.html. Many
      more such incidents can be found at the Web site of the Foundation for Individual
      Rights in Education (FIRE) at http://www.thefire.org/index.php/.
11   18 U.S.C. § 249. See United States Department of Justice, Civil Rights Division Web
      page at: http://www.justice.gov/crt/crim/249fin.php.
12   Conversation with the author in June 2000, following the Supreme Court hearing.
13   United States Crime Rates 1960—2008, from FBI Uniform Crime Reports,
      summarized at: http://www.disastercenter.com/crime/uscrime.htm.
14   2008 Hate Crime Statistics, FBI, Table 1, at: http://www.fbi.gov/ucr/hc2008/data/

table_01.html.

15 "Rightwing Extremism: Current Economic and Political Climate Fueling Resurgence in Radicalization and Recruitment," Department of Homeland Security, April 7, 2009, at: http://www.fas.org/irp/eprint/rightwing.pdf.

16 Rory Leishman, "Canadian Human Rights Tribunals Should Be Ditched," *London* (Ontario, Canada) *Free Press*, as reprinted on July 11, 2001, at http://www.cwfa.org/articles/110/CFI/cfreport.

17 "Canadian Teacher Harassed for Expressing Personal Views on Homosexuality," the National Association of Research and Therapy of Homosexuality (NARTH), Feb. 8, 2008, at: http://www.narth.com/docs/canteacher.html.

18 Hilary White, "Mark Steyn Case Wakes Up Canadian Press to Human Rights Tribunals' Threat to Free Speech," LifesiteNews, Dec. 19, 2007, at: http://www.lifesitenews.com/ldn/2007/dec/07121902.html.

19 Video of the mob scene is at http://www.massresistance.org/docs/gen/09b/ParkStreetChurch_0428/index.html.

20 Bipartisan Campaign Reform Act of 2002, Public Law 107-155, at: http://www.law.cornell.edu/background/campaign_finance/bcra_txt.pdf.

21 Seth McLaughlin, "Supreme Court Overturns Key Part of McCain-Feingold," *Human Events*, Jan. 21, 2010, at: http://www.humanevents.com/article.php?id=35287.

22 *Citizens United vs. Federal Election Commission* (2010), at: http://www.law.cornell.edu/supct/html/08-205.ZS.html.

23 The Democracy Is Strengthened by Casting Light on Spending in Elections Act (HR 5175), at: http://www.govtrack.us/congress/bill.xpd?bill=h111-5175.

24 Jill Jackson, "House Passes DISCLOSE ACT," CBSNEWS.com, June 24, 2010, at: http://www.cbsnews.com/8301-503544_162-20008783-503544.html.

25 Greg Hitt and Brody Mullins, "Contribution-Disclosure Measure Fails Senate Test Vote," *The Wall Street Journal* online, July 27, 2010, at: http://online.wsj.com/article/SB10001424052748703977004575393541649256712.html?mod=googlenews_wsj.

26 As quoted in David R. Sands, "Senate vote rejects Fairness Doctrine revival," *The Washington Times*, February 27, 2008, p. A-6.

27 Brian Fitzpatrick, "Unmasking the Myths Behind the Fairness Doctrine," Culture and Media Institute, Media Research Center, June 10, 2008, pp. 8-16.

28 Ibid, p. 12.

29 Benjamin Toff, "Ratings: 'CBS Evening News' in Prime Time Averages 6.5 million viewers," *The New York Times* TV Decoder column, Jan. 29, 2009, at: http://tvdecoder.blogs.nytimes.com/2009/01/29/ratings-cbs-evening-news-in-prime-time-averages-65-million-viewers, and State of the News Media 2009 at http://www.stateofthenewsmedia.org/2009/narrative_networktv_audience.php?media=6&cat=2#NetAudEveView.

30 *The Structural Imbalance of Political Talk Radio*, a joint project of the Center for American Progress and the Free Press, June 21 and 22, 2007, at: http://www.americanprogress.org/issues/2007/06/pdf/talk_radio.pdf.

31 Cliff Kincaid, "Controversial New Video of Obama's Pastor," Accuracy in Media,

Nov. 1, 2009, at: http://www.aim.org/aim-column/controversial-new-video-of-obamas-pastor/.

32   Ibid.

33   Ibid.

34   Matt Cover, "FCC's Diversity Officer Wants Private Broadcasters to Pay a Sum Equal to Their Total Operating Costs to Fund Public Broadcasting," CNSNews.com, August 12, 2009, at: http://www.cnsnews.com/news/article/52435, and *Structural Imbalance*, op. cit, p. 2.

Chapter Eleven

1   Fidel Castro, quoted in Paul Haven, "Dubious endorsement: Cuban leader endorses U.S. health care reform, says it's about time," Associated Press, March 25, 2010.

2   Erika Bolstad, "Alaska joins states' suit against federal health care overrule," *Anchorage Daily News*, April 21, 2010, at: http://www.adn.com/2010/04/20/1241989/alaska-to-join-states-health-bill.html.

3   J. Kenneth Blackwell and Kenneth A. Klukowski, "Why the ObamaCare Tax Penalty Is Unconstitutional," *The Wall Street Journal*, July 22, 2010, p. A-19.

4   Bret Stephens, "Dr. Berwick and That Fabulous Cuban Health Care," *The Wall Street Journal*, July 13, 2010, p. A-17.

5   Mark Steyn, "A healthy dose of catastrophe: As government grows, prosperity dwindles," *The Washington Times*, March 29, 2010, p. B-4.

6   "The ObamaCare Writedowns—II, editorial, *The Wall Street Journal*, March 31, 2010, p. A-22.

7   Timothy P. Cahill, "Massachusetts Is Our Future," *The Wall Street Journal*, March 26, 2010, p. A-19.

8   "Stark, Woolsey, Schakowsky" Introduce Public Option Act," press release, office of Pete Stark, July 22, 2010, at: http://www.stark.house.gov/index.php?option=com_content&task=view&id=2010&Itemid=62&doc=interstitialskip.

9   Mark Steyn, "Obamacare worth the price to Democrats," *Orange County Register*, March 5, 2010, at: http://www.ocregister.com/articles/health-237719-care-government.html.

10   Quoted in Steyn, Ibid.

11   Public Law 111-148, at: http://www.gpo.gov/fdsys/pkg/PLAW-111publ148/content-detail.html.

12   W. Douglas Elmendorf, director, Congressional Budget Office, letter to Sen. Harry Reid, March 11, 2010, at: http://www.cbo.gov/ftpdocs/113xx/doc11307/Reid_Letter_HR3590.pdf.

13   Michael D. Tanner, "Bad Medicine: A Guide to the Real Costs and Consequences of the New Health Care Law," Cato Institute White Paper, July 12, 2010, at: http://www.cato.org/pub_display.php?pub_id=11961.

14   "IRS Expansion," FactCheck.org, the Annenberg Public Policy Center, March 30, 2010, at: http://www.factcheck.org/2010/03/irs-expansion/.

15   David S. Hilsenrath, "Health-care law may pose challenges for IRS, taxpayers," *The Washington Post*, July 7, 2010, at: http://www.washingtonpost.com/wp-dyn/

content/article/2010/07/07/AR2010070702826.html.

16   David G. Green, Laura Casper, Delay, Institute of Economic Affairs (London), *Delay, Denial and Dilution: The Impact of NHS Rationing on Heart Disease and Cancer* (Suffolk, England: St. Emundsbury Press, 2000), p. 8, at: http://www.liberty-page.com/issues/healthcare/rationreport.pdf.

17   Ibid, p. 12

18   Janet Adamy, "Hints on Public Health-Insurance Plan," *The Wall Street Journal* Washington Wire, April 24, 2009, at: http://blogs.wsj.com/washwire/2009/04/24/hints-on-public-health-insurance-plan/

19   Marc Siegel, M.D., "When Doctors Opt Out: We Already Know What Government-Run Health Care Looks Like," *The Wall Street Journal*, April 17, 2009, at: http://online.wsj.com/article/SB123993462778328019.html.

20   David Leonhardt, "After the Great Recession," *The New York Times Sunday Magazine*, May 3, 2009, at: http://www.nytimes.com/2009/05/03/magazine/03Obama-t.html?pagewanted=6&_r=1&ref=magazine.

21   "Obama's health care rationing," *The Washington Times*, May 1, 2009, at: http://www.washingtontimes.com/news/2009/may/01/obamas-health-care-rationing/.

22   Dan Springer, "Oregon Offers Terminal Patients Doctor-Assisted Suicide Instead of Medical Care," FoxNews.com, July 28, 2008, at: http://www.foxnews.com/story/0,2933,392962,00.html.

23   Ibid.

24   Ibid.

25   Ibid.

26   Health Care Law—Rasmussen Reports, July 28, 2010, at: http://www.rasmussenreports.com/public_content/politics/current_events/healthcare/health_care_law.

Chapter Twelve

1   "Bush Deficit vs. Obama Deficit in Pictures," Heritage Foundation, March 24, 2009, at: http://blog.heritage.org/2009/03/24/bush-deficit-vs-obama-deficit-in-pictures/.

2   Quoted in "Obamanomics," editorial, *The Washington Times*, March 16, 2009, at: http://www.washingtontimes.com/news/2009/mar/16/obamanomics/.

3   Julie Mason, "Obama's spending splurge confounds D.C.'s establishment", *Washington Examiner*, March 8, 2009, at: http://www.washingtonexaminer.com/politics/Obamas-spending-splurge-confounds-DCs-establishment---40931977.html.

4   Brian M. Riedl, "The Obama Budget: Spending, Taxes, and Doubling the National Debt," *Backgrounder* #2249, March 16, 2009, at: http://www.heritage.org/Research/Budget/bg2249.cfm

5   Bureau of Labor Statistics cited by Veronique de Rugy, "Private Sector Losses, Public Sector Gains," the Corner, *National Review* online, June 24, 2010, at: http://corner.nationalreview.com/post/?q=MDkwMzA0YzJlNTIzMWUxZmI4MTA4YmU0YmEwOWI0ZmI.

6   Husna Haq, "Unemployment rate: 9.7 percent. Underemployment: far higher," *Christian Science Monitor*, March 5, 2010, at: http://www.csmonitor.com/

Money/2010/0305/Unemployment-rate-9.7-percent.-Underemployment-far-higher.

7   "2009 Pig Book Summary," Citizens Against Government Waste, at: http://www. cagw.org/site/PageServer?pagename=reports_pigbook2009.

8   David A. Patten, "Economists: Federal Spending Spins 'Out of Control' Under Obama," *Newsmax*, March 17, 2009, at: http://www.newsmax.com/newsfront/obama_economists_debt/2009/03/17/192995.html.

9   Quoted in Patten.

10 "Before devotees of our prince-president start reaching for their pitchforks and tar buckets, let's be clear that the brand of national socialism now being practiced in Washington has nothing to do with the capital-lettered National Socialism that drove the horrible Hitler regime or the equally disgraceful brands of big-F Fascism practiced by Mussolini, Franco, Peron, and other despots of the last century and this. Schacht himself was a stiff-necked and bumptiously offensive self-promoter but he was never a Nazi, a fact Hitler himself recognized by putting him in a concentration camp toward the war's end." James Srodes, "The National Socialism of Obamanomics," *The American Spectator*, May 2009, at: http://spectator.org/archives/2009/05/01/the-national-socialism-of-obam.

11 Ibid.

12 Ian Talley, "EPA Poised to Declare C02 a Public Danger," *The Wall Street Journal*, December 5, 2009, at: http://online.wsj.com/article/NA_WSJ_PUB:SB126003232518778287.html.

13 Michelle Malkin, "Senate Showdown Over EPA Power Grab," Michelle Malkin's blog, June 10, 2010, at: http://michellemalkin.com/2010/06/10/senate-showdown-over-epa-power-grab/.

14 "Obamanomics," editorial, *The Washington Times*, March 16, 2009, at: http://www.washingtontimes.com/news/2009/mar/16/obamanomics/.

Chapter Thirteen

1   Phyllis Schlafly, "'Equal Rights' for Women: Wrong Then, Wrong Now," *Los Angeles Times*, April 8, 2007, at: http://www.latimes.com/news/opinion/la-op-schafly8apr08,0,6143259.story.

2   Scott Somerville, Esq., "The Politics of Survival: Home Schoolers and the Law," Home School Legal Defense Association, at: http://www.hslda.org/docs/nche/000010/PoliticsofSurvival.asp.

3   "Senate immigration bill suffers crushing defeat," CNN, at: http://www.cnn.com/2007/POLITICS/06/28/immigration.congress/index.html

4   Quoted in Matt Barber, "The foul face of 'gay activism,'" OneNewsNow, April 24, 2009, at: http://www.onenewsnow.com/Perspectives/Default.aspx?id=502680.

5   Ibid.

6   John Fund, Political Diary newsletter, excerpted in Notable & Quotable, *The Wall Street Journal*, July 21, 2010, p. A-17.

7   "Dan Rather's Liberal Bias," Media Research Center, 2005, at: http://www.mrc.org/projects/rather20th/welcome.asp.

8   Lydia Sand, "Congress Ranks Last in Confidence in Institutions," Gallup, Inc.,

July 22, 2010, at: http://www.gallup.com/poll/141512/Congress-Ranks-Last-Confidence-Institutions.aspx?ve.

9   "Pajamas TV Final Estimate: April 15 Tea Party Attendance Exceeded One Million," press release, April 30, 2009, at: Thttp://news.yahoo.com/s/usnw/20090430/pl_usnw/pajamas_tv_final_estimate__april15_tea_party_attendance_exceeded_one_million.

10   Charlie Martin, "March on Washington: How Big Was the Crowd?" Pajamas Media, Sept. 14, 2009, at: http://pajamasmedia.com/blog/how-big-was-the-crowd/.

11   Jake Tapper, "President Obama Says Arizona's "Poorly-Conceived" Immigration Law Could Mean Hispanic-Americans Are Harassed," ABCNews.com, April 27, 2010, at: http://blogs.abcnews.com/politicalpunch/2010/04/president-obama-says-arizonas-poorlyconceived-immigration-law-could-mean-hispanicamericans-are-haras.html.

12   Noel Sheppard, "Attorney General Holder Admits He's Never Read Arizona Law," Newsbusters.org, May 13, 2010, at: http://newsbusters.org/blogs/noel-sheppard/2010/05/13/attorney-general-holder-admits-never-reading-arizonas-immigration-law. Also, "Napolitano Admits She Hasn't Read Arizona Law But Says She Wouldn't Sign It," Real Clear Politics Video, May 17, 2010, at: http://www.realclearpolitics.com/video/2010/05/17/napolitano_admits_she_hasnt_read_arizona_law_but_says_she_wouldnt_sign_it.html.

13   Julia Preston, "Justice Dept. Sues Arizona Over Its Immigration Law," *The New York Times*, July 6, 2010, at: http://www.nytimes.com/2010/07/07/us/07immig.html.

14   Stephen Dinan and Kara Rowland, "Justice: Sanctuary cities safe from law," *The Washington Times*, July 14, 2010, at: http://www.washingtontimes.com/news/2010/jul/14/justice-sanctuary-cities-are-no-arizona/.

15   "NAACP Delegates Vote to Repudiate Racist Elements Within Tea Party," press release, NAACP Website, at: http://www.naacp.org/news/entry/naacp-delegates-vote-to-repudiate-racist-elements-within-the-tea-pary/.

16   Chelsea Schilling, "'Want Freedom? Kill some crackers!'" WorldNetDaily.com, July 7, 2010, at: http://www.wnd.com/?pageId=175817.

17   Ibid.

18   J. Christian Adams, "Inside the Black Panther Case," op-ed, *The Washington Times*, June 25, 2010, at: http://www.washingtontimes.com/news/2010/jun/25/inside-the-black-panther-case-anger-ignorance-and-/.

19   "New Black Panther Party: Will Justice Department Investigate Julie Fernandes?" *The Foundry*, Heritage Foundation, July 9, 2010, at: http://blog.heritage.org/2010/07/09/new-black-panther-party-will-justice-department-investigate-julie-fernandes/.

20   Calvin Coolidge, quoted in William J. Federer, *Three Secular Reasons Why America Should Be Under God* (St. Louis: Amerisearch, Inc., 2008), p. 35.

INDEX

W

ABOUT THE AUTHOR

ROBERT KNIGHT is Senior Writer/Correspondent for Coral Ridge Ministries. Mr. Knight formerly directed the Media Research Center's Culture and Media Institute, and is currently a Senior Fellow for the American Civil Rights Union.

He frequently appears on television and radio, and is published and quoted in newspapers and magazines. Topics of special interest are media bias, religious freedom, and family-related issues.

Mr. Knight directed the Culture & Family Institute at Concerned Women for America (2001-2006), founded and directed the Cultural Studies Program at the Family Research Council (1992-2001) and was a senior fellow at the Heritage Foundation (1990-1991). He wrote and directed two video documentaries: *Hidden Truth: What You Deserve to Know About Abortion,* and *The Children of Table 34,* about sex research pioneer Alfred C. Kinsey's crimes against children.

He was a news editor and writer for the *Los Angeles Times* (1982-1989), and a Media Fellow at Stanford University's Hoover Institution (1989-1990). He was weekend projects coordinator at the Fort Lauderdale *Sun-Sentinel* (1980-1982), a reporter for the Annapolis *Evening Capital,* assistant editor of its sister paper, the *Maryland Gazette* (1978-1980), and a reporter and editor at the *Maryland Coast Press* (1975-1978).

A draftsman of the federal Defense of Marriage Act, Knight was instrumental in its passage in 1996 and the defeat of the Employment Non-Discrimination Act. He was honored with Family Research Council's Faith, Family and Freedom award in

2001. He is the author of *Radical Rulers: The White House Elites Who Are Pushing America Toward Socialism, The Silencers: How Liberals Are Trying to Shut Down Media Freedom in the U.S.* (Coral Ridge Ministries, 2010), and *The Age of Consent: The Rise of Relativism and the Corruption of Popular Culture* (Spence Publishing, 1998, 2000). He frequently debates and speaks on college campuses, including appearances at UC Berkeley, Cornell, Kent State, North Carolina State, Liberty University, and others.

Mr. Knight has a Master's degree and a Bachelor of Science degree in Political Science from American University. He lives in northern Virginia with his wife and children and they attend a non-denominational, Bible-based church.

FIGHTING FOR
AMERICA'S SOUL